How to Sell
COLLECTIBLES
on eBay

Other Entrepreneur Pocket Guides include

How to Sell Clothing, Shoes, and Accessories on eBay

How to Sell Toys and Hobbies on eBay

Start Your Real Estate Career

Start Your Restaurant Career

Entrepreneur
MAGAZINE'S
POCKET GUIDES

How to Sell
COLLECTIBLES
on eBay

Entrepreneur Press and
Jennifer A. Ericsson

EP
Entrepreneur.
Press

Editorial Director: Jere L. Calmes
Cover Design: Beth Hansen-Winter
Production and Composition: Eliot House Productions

This publication is designed to provide accurate and authoritative information in regard to the subject matter covered. It is sold with the understanding that the publisher is not engaged in rendering legal, accounting or
other professional services. If legal advice or other expert assistance is
required, the services of a competent professional person should be sought.

Library of Congress Cataloging-in-Publication Data is available.

ISBN: 1599180-04-9

Printed in Canada
12 11 10 09 08 07 06   10 9 8 7 6 5 4 3 2 1

Contents

Preface and Acknowledgments xiii

Chapter 1

What Is a Collectible?. 1

Who Are Collectors? 2

Spotlight on Steiff Bears 3

Collectible Age Categories. 4

Spotlight on Ty Beanie Babies 5

Will Vintage and Modern Collectibles Become Antiques? . . 6

Availability 7

Value 7

A Dr. Seuss E-Value-Ation 9

Who Makes Collectibles and
　　What Purpose Do They Serve? 10

eBay and Collectibles 10

Chapter 2
eBay Selling 101 11
Registering as a User 12
My eBay Page 13
About Me Page 13
Setting Up an eBay Seller Account 14
The Selling Process 15
Feedback 16
Seller Profiles 17
Spotlight on Fiestaware 19
Spotlight on Madame Alexander Dolls 21
Spotlight on Coca Cola 22
Many Kinds of eBay Sellers 25

Chapter 3
Own What They Want 27
Spotlight on Fenton Glass 28
Demand 28
Becoming an Expert 29
Finding Inventory 31
Spotlight on Disneyana 31
How Much to Spend 34
Spending Mistakes 35
Spotlight on Signed Baseballs 36
Main Collectible eBay Categories 37

Chapter 4
To Auction or Not 39
Traditional Auctions 39
Reserve Price Auction 40
Buy It Now (BIN) 40
Spotlight on Hummel/Goebel 41
Fixed-Price Listings 42
Private Auctions. 42
Dutch Auctions 43
Live Auctions. 44
Restricted-Access Auctions. 44
Spotlight on DC Comics 45
Want It Now 46
Best Offer 46
Spotlight on Longaberger 47
eBay Stores. 48
eBay Express 48

Chapter 5
Proper Pricing 49
eBay Fees 49
Value 50
Helpful eBay Research Tools 51
A Word About Price Guides. 52
Spotlight on Waterman Pens. 53
Pricing an Auction 54
Fixed-Price Listing 57

Spotlight on Lladro Ceramics 58

Chapter 6

Winning Listings 59

Determine Your Starting Price 59

Spotlight on Art Deco Posters 62

Common Collectible Condition Problems 64

Listing Strategies 66

Spotlight on Nodders 69

Chapter 7

Customer Care 71

How to Provide Great Customer Service 72

Spotlight on Landers, Frary & Clark Kitchenware 75

Importance of Packing and Shipping 77

Spotlight on Perfume Bottles 77

Chapter 8

Getting Started 85

Part Time vs. Full Time 86

Location 86

Spotlight on Royal Doulton Collectible Plates 88

Start-Up Expenses 89

Ongoing Expenses 92

Spotlight on Singer Featherweight Sewing Machines 94

Collectible Business Chores 95

Chapter 9

Expanding Through eBay Tools 99

About Me Page 99

eBay Store. 100

Spotlight on Mandarin Garnets 101

Trading Assistants 106

eBay PowerSeller Program 107

Auction Management Tools 108

Marketplace Research. 109

eBay Pulse 109

Spotlight on Star Wars Merchandise 110

What's Hot by Category 111

Chapter 10

Finding Your Customer Base 113

Why Will a Customer Buy from You? 114

eBay Promotional Tools 115

Spotlight on Pinball Machines 116

Spotlight on Political Memorabilia 118

Create Your Personal Web Site 119

Take Out an Ad 119

Spotlight on Postage Stamps 120

Build a Customer Mailing List 121

Networking with Other Collectors and Sellers 122

Chapter 11

Keeping Track of Your Collectibles 123

Purchasing Collectibles 123

Spotlight on Riihimaen Lasi Oy Glass 124

Spotlight on Lead Toy Soldiers 127

Staying Organized 129

Chapter 12

Money Matters 133

Choosing a Legal Form of Business 133

Spotlight on Seth Thomas Clocks 135

Keeping Track of Income and Expenses 137

Spotlight on Pez Dispensers 138

Record-Keeping 139

Financial Management. 140

Controlling Expenses. 143

Forecasting for the Future 143

Chapter 13

Hiring Help. 145

Employee vs. Independent Contractor 145

Job Application 147

Spotlight on Emerson Electric Fans 148

Where Are Your Future Employees? 149

Evaluating Applicants. 149

Once They're on Board 151

Employee Benefits. 152

Short-Term Solutions. 152

Workers' Compensation Insurance 153

Spotlight on Collectible Swords. 153

Termination 154

Chapter 14
You've Only Just Begun **155**

Collectibles and eBay 156

A Worldwide Experience 156

It's Not as Overwhelming as It Seems 157

Spotlight on McDonalds Happy Meal Toys 158

WOW! Sales 160

Is the Collectible Market Strong?. 161

Appendix
Resource Guide **163**

Online Price Guides. 163

Online Auction Management Services 164

Online Appraisals. 165

Collecting Publications. 165

Wholesale Equipment and Supplies. 166

Online Book Stores 167

Book Price Guides. 167

Additional Titles. 168

Collecting Clubs and Associations. 168

Glossary. 173

Index 177

Preface and
Acknowledgments

*W*hen I first started writing this book, I knew very little about collectibles or eBay. I worried that perhaps I wasn't the best person for the project because I wasn't an expert on either of these topics. As soon as I started researching, I realized how much I didn't know. I couldn't tell you the difference between a vintage collectible and an antique. I had no idea what MIB or BIN meant. And grading? Well, that was something I remembered from college.

After some momentary panic at the scope and magnitude of both collectibles and eBay, it occurred to me that maybe I was the perfect person to write this guide. After all, if a non-expert like me could learn and explain the process, then anyone interested in selling collectibles on eBay could do it, too.

Today I am confident that a vintage collectible is at least 25 years old but not yet over 100, the legal qualifier for an antique. If I see a listing on eBay that is marked MIB and BIN, I know it is mint-in-box and I can buy it right now. If that same item has been graded, then I know there is an accurate accounting of its true condition. I am no longer intimidated by eBay, and I know an incredible amount of information about collectibles.

This pocket guide provides an overview on how to sell modern and vintage collectibles on eBay. It does not include antiques, as they require a book of their own. Early chapters take you from a definition of collectibles to how to find, research, and sell them on eBay. Middle chapters focus on the different types of eBay auctions available, the best ways to price and list items, the important aspects of packing and shipping, and customer care essentials. Later chapters introduce ways to expand your business through eBay tools and other basic business matters like setting up an office, record-keeping, money matters, and hiring employees. Throughout the book, successful eBay sellers from around the country share helpful advice.

Certainly, I did not write this book alone. My primary function for this project was as a writer, not an eBay seller. I needed insight from experienced people who dealt in collectibles on eBay every day. I would like to acknowledge the following eBay sellers who assisted me in this project: Jane Moen of Iowa, Kathy Shaughnessy of Texas, Cindy and Larry Brown of Missouri, Scott Gaynor of Massachusetts, Sam Buchanan of California, and especially Beth Titus of New

Hampshire. They graciously put aside their suspicions when a stranger approached wanting to ask them all kinds of questions about their eBay businesses. They took time out of their busy days to respond to my inquiries and shared their eBay and collectibles experiences. I am grateful for their cooperation and candid responses. I certainly couldn't have done this book without them!

What Is a
Collectible?

*I*F YOU ASKED THREE PEOPLE THE DEFINITION OF A COL-
lectible, you would probably get three different answers. The housewife who buys cookie jars
to decorate her kitchen might tell you that a collectible is something
you buy for fun. The athlete who collects Olympic memorabilia
might say that it is an item that is rare and hard to find. The gentle-
man who purchases gold coins might insist that a collectible is
something whose value will increase over time. Collectibles can
definitely be all of these things; however, they don't have to be. In
fact, any item could be considered a collectible as long as people
are choosing to acquire it.

Who Are Collectors?

Collectors are an incredibly diverse group. They come from all ethnic and socioeconomic backgrounds. They live all over the world, speaking many different languages. Some acquired the collecting bug early in life, whereas others have recently discovered the joys of accumulation. Generally these individuals can be divided into two major groups—the casual collectors and the serious collectors.

Casual Collectors

The casual collector is a person who sees something they like and buys it. For them, collecting is an enjoyable hobby. They are not buying their collectibles for investment purposes or with the intent to resell them. They don't worry about how rare or valuable the items might be. If the object pleases them, then it must be a good purchase.

A casual collector may purchase things that seem ridiculous to serious collectors. For instance, some people collect frogs. They have massive quantities of frog knickknacks and whatnots. You or I might think this collection a bunch of worthless junk, but a quick search on eBay shows that there are plenty of people who love frogs. There were 63 current listings for frog banks, candles, teapots, pens, cookie jars, plush toys, watches, and figurines—and people were buying them.

Enjoyment can come from some very strange places. eBay has a Weird Stuff category where I immediately found three items that could be considered collectible. First, there was a key from Alcatraz with 28 bids, the high one at $61. Secondly, there was a six-inch frog car decal—perfect for the collectors mentioned earlier. It was going for $7 with five bidders. Last was my personal favorite, a listing titled "Scary Old Early 1900s Steiff Bear with Issues." That certainly got my atten-

SPOTLIGHT ON STEIFF BEARS

In 1907, the Steiff bear craze hit its peak with the German factory producing 974,000 bears a year, most of which were exported to the United States. These stuffed bears had gotten great American exposure at the 1904 St. Louis World's Fair where children and adults alike fell in love with them. These high-quality teddy bears were identified by the button sewn in their ear stamped with the Steiff name. Different colors of bears were produced, with black ones being the rarest kind.

In 2006, a miniature, 3½-inch chocolate brown mohair Steiff teddy from the 1950s sold for $114.50. In addition, a 13-inch bear from 1906 fetched $1,050.09. These examples are only two of the 504 current Steiff listings. The continued production and popularity of these bears enables Steiff to be the premier bear collectible name. Oh yes, the Scary Steiff bear mentioned in the text brought its seller $161.14 in spite of the fact that it was missing an eye and was in desperate need of restoration!

tion, and buyers were outbidding each other to try to purchase this strange bear that the seller had locked in the trunk of her car!

Serious Collectors

The serious collector is an entirely different breed of collector. The serious collector believes there are other factors to consider when determining what items qualify as collectibles, including an item's age, availability, and value. For them, a collectible must stand the test of time, be of a limited quantity, and hold some sort of value, whether it is historical, aesthetic, or intrinsic.

Many serious collectors believe that it takes about 25 years for an item to prove itself in the collectible market. Until enough time has passed, it is hard to determine which things will become significant and which items will be forgotten. Simply because something is "hot" today, does not mean it will remain popular forever. Beanie Babies are a good example of this.

Collectible Age Categories

The collectibles of today can be separated into three different categories based on their age. There are modern collectibles, vintage collectibles, and antique collectibles.

Modern Collectibles

Modern collectibles, like the Beanie Babies, are items that have become popular in the recent past or are of current interest.

SPOTLIGHT ON TY BEANIE BABIES

In 1996, anyone with an elementary school-aged child was well aware of the craze that swept the nation with these small, inexpensive stuffed toys. They went from being the perfect birthday party gift to a "must have" item for children and adults alike. Many parents believed they could finance their child's college education if they kept the ones they bought in mint condition with the tags. Of course, to do that, their children were never allowed to play with them. Prices soared from the reasonable $5 to an outrageous $50 or more.

In 2006, a search of Beanie Babies on eBay shows 16,288 current listings and a whopping 38,343 completed listings. At first that might seem like a good sign; unfortunately, when you look closer at the completed auctions, most of the items didn't sell, even though they were reasonably priced between $.99 and $6.99. The only Beanies that were hot were the early ones like a Lizzy that went for $66 and a Bumble the Bee that sold for $61. One seller was trying to unload a lot of 100 retired Beanies with a starting bid of $195. There were no takers. I certainly hope her child had not just been admitted to Harvard!

American Girl dolls, Hello Kitty glassware, or a Star Wars Darth Vader clock radio would all fit into this category. In general, these collectibles are less than 25 years old.

Vintage Collectibles

Vintage collectibles represent a previous time or era. These items are more than 25 years old, but are not yet antiques. LP records from the 1960s are an example of a vintage collectible, as is a Madame Alexander Dionne Quintuplet doll from the 1930s or a Panasonic Toot-o-Loop radio from the 1970s.

Antique Collectibles

Antiques have historical and artistic value, and generally fall into one of four main categories—ceramics, furniture, glass, and metalwork. Some things, like your great-grandmother's silver baby spoon, could be considered both a collectible and an antique. A Shaker chair, a Tiffany lamp, and a Tucker pitcher are other examples of items that qualify as both antiques and collectibles. For the most part, these items are more than 100 years old. Though some collectors may argue this point, the U.S. government uses the century mark for declaring something legally an antique.

Will Vintage and Modern Collectibles Become Antiques?

Given enough time, some vintage and modern collectibles may become antiques, but most of them won't. For instance, the plastic lava lamp you purchased last week may not hold up over the next century to earn a place next to a kerosene lamp from the 1860s. Or that Millennium Swatch you sport on your wrist may never garner you the same price at auction as a silver pocket watch from Victorian times. Only time will tell.

Availability

Availability is the second factor that serious collectors look at when evaluating collectibles. When an item is first produced, supply is plentiful. Customers have no trouble finding it, and they are happy to own it. A collectible is born when these same customers decide that they want more of this item and it is no longer readily available. For most collectibles, there is a limited supply that is continually decreasing. As time passes there are fewer and fewer items and, hopefully, the demand and value of these items increases.

Value

The third factor that serious collectors consider when looking at collectibility is value. There are different kinds of value to consider when determining the true worth of any particular item. Only one of these is monetary. The others are historical value, aesthetic value, intrinsic value, celebrity value, and sentimental value. A collectible may have one or more of these values.

Historical Value

Items that are important from our past have historical value. Antiques inherently have this type of value, but a recent example might be memorabilia from the 2004 World Series that the Boston Red Sox finally won. In any case, collectors will pay more for items with historical value.

Aesthetic Value

Items that are artistic or beautiful have aesthetic value. A Weller vase or a Royal Copenhagen figurine are examples of this type of value. Many collectors purchase the items they do because they are pleasing to the eye.

Intrinsic Value

Items made of costly materials have intrinsic value. Gold watches or gemstone jewelry are examples of things that are intrinsically valuable. Collectors know that these items will not come cheap.

Celebrity Value

Anything owned, used, or affiliated with someone famous has celebrity value. An LP signed by all the Beatles, a Joe Namath football jersey, or even one of Paris Hilton's handbags would all certainly possess celebrity value. Any collector interested in these items would pay top dollar.

Sentimental Value

Any item that someone holds near and dear to their heart would have sentimental value. Never discount sentimental value. An object can be priceless to a person with an emotional attachment to it. It doesn't matter whether it's a doll they remember from their childhood, a milk glass vase from their grandmother, or the poster from the best Doors concert they ever attended. Whatever it is, if it has special meaning, then that collector will want it—no matter what.

Monetary Value

Simply stated, monetary value is how much money someone is willing to pay for an item. For the collector, no matter which type, how wide they open their wallets will likely depend on one or all of these many types of value.

A DR. SEUSS E-VALUE-ATION

If I own a signed, first-edition copy of the picture book, *And to Think That I Saw it On Mulberry Street*, by Theodore Geisel (otherwise known as Dr. Seuss), is it valuable? It was published in 1937 and is in mint condition. Because Dr. Seuss was, and still is, one of the most beloved and successful children's authors of all time, this book would have not only historical and aesthetic value, but also celebrity value. Made of paper, it may not have any intrinsic value, but its great sentimental value should push its monetary value, or what someone would pay for it, quite high.

Who Makes Collectibles and What Purpose Do They Serve?

It is impossible to name all the manufacturers of collectible items. In an effort to familiarize you with at least some of them, you will find Spotlights, like the ones on Steiff and Beanie Babies in this chapter, throughout the book. Look for collectible names such as Fenton Glass, Longaberger Baskets, Disneyana, and Waterman Pens. Each Spotlight will start with an important date from the past and end with a present-day eBay report for that collectible.

The purpose of collectibles is different for everyone. In the majority of cases, collectibles are purchased to be displayed in some manner. They might be on bookshelves, in cases or cabinets, set out on tables, or kept under glass. The collectors are their primary caretakers, in charge of dusting, polishing, and preserving the items until they are ready to part with them. And, at that point, they just might decide that eBay is the place to sell them.

eBay and Collectibles

No one has a crystal ball that will say what collectible items will be in demand next month, next year, or 20 years down the road. The collectible market is fluid and ever changing, and so is eBay. eBay is constantly being updated to accommodate the buyers and sellers that use it. If you are considering selling collectibles, then eBay is an outlet you should explore.

eBay
Selling 101

*T*O SELL COLLECTIBLES ON EBAY, YOU MUST HAVE A working knowledge of the particular items you want to sell and of the way the eBay system works. This chapter will familiarize you with eBay and the selling process, as well as introduce you to six established eBay sellers willing to share their experiences and insights into this amazing online world. The first time you connect to the eBay site, it can be overwhelming. There is so much out there, and much of it you don't understand. Take things slowly until you get used to the way eBay works. Soon, you will be much less intimidated.

Registering as a User

The first step is to register as a user. It is a simple procedure and eBay prompts you each step of the way. You will be asked to provide your name, address, telephone number, and e-mail address. You will also be asked to create a unique eBay user ID and password. You will be shown the eBay User Agreement and Privacy Policy. It is quite lengthy, but print it, read it, and then agree to its terms. To complete your registration, confirm the e-mail that eBay sends to you. Although you can browse the eBay site without registering, you may not bid, see selling prices, buy, or sell until you have completed the process.

Your eBay User ID

Choose your eBay user ID thoughtfully. This is the name under which your reputation as a buyer and seller will be established. Though it's possible to change your user ID, it's not always a good idea. If you change your user ID, people who have done business with you before may not be able to find you by searching using your old user ID. Another drawback of changing your user ID is that you get a "name change" icon next to your new user ID for 30 days, and that could make some new potential buyers suspicious. One good thing about changing your user ID is that your history follows you, and your feedback remains intact, so any reputation you've worked hard to build will come with you no matter what your user ID is.

When choosing your user ID, consider the image it's likely to project to prospective customers and be sure that image is one you want to portray. Your user ID should also be easy to remember. A combination of letters and numbers that might make perfect sense to you (say, the first two letters of each of your children's names, followed by their birth months) could be hard-to-remember gibberish to someone else.

Sellers often make a mistake with their original user ID and want to change it later, but they may be reluctant because they don't want their customers to lose track of them. However, buyers who have marked you as a "favorite seller" will have your new name automatically updated on their My eBay page.

My eBay Page

Every registered user has their own place where they can keep track of all their current and recent eBay activities. From your My eBay page, you can view all the items you are bidding on or watching, have recently purchased or sold, or have listed to sell. You can look up your favorite searches, sellers, or eBay stores. You can also check your eBay finances, or read feedback that other buyers and sellers have left about you from this page. This is your home base in the eBay world. Do not confuse it with your About Me page.

About Me Page

You have the opportunity to create a special page on eBay where you tell people about yourself and your business.

> **TIP**
>
> Before you start selling on eBay, you might want to experiment as a Buyer first so that you understand both ends of any transaction. The only way to really get familiar with eBay is to use it. Do some searching. Bid on a few items. Win an auction or two. Correspond with sellers. Pay for and receive some items. Leave and get feedback of your own. In addition, use the many informational links that eBay provides to help you learn the site as quickly as possible. You will be a better Seller because of it.

Buyers will see the Me icon next to your user ID if you have designed this page. Many sellers choose not to post personal information here; however, if the page is done well, it may improve your sales. More information on the About Me page is offered in Chapter 9.

Setting Up an eBay Seller Account

Once you are a registered user, you can then create an eBay Seller Account so you can begin to sell items on eBay. To do this, you will have to provide eBay with your personal bank account and credit card information. There are fees involved with each eBay transaction, and you will need to decide how you are going to pay them. You will be authorizing eBay to make deductions from your account or charge your credit card to cover these fees.

The Selling Process

Although each selling experience will be slightly different, the process you go through for each collectible is largely the same. First, you'll need to decide which items to sell. You'll need to research your collectibles so that you know exactly what you have, and what they are worth. Next, you'll need to take quality digital photographs and write accurate descriptions of the items. You'll also need to determine the shipping costs by weighing each item in its packing material. Once you have done these things, you'll be ready to list the collectible on eBay.

While you are listing your collectibles on eBay, you will determine the length of your auctions and your accepted payment methods. During the auctions, you'll answer any e-mails you get from potential bidders. If your item sells, you'll contact the buyers and arrange for payment. After payment is received, you'll carefully pack and ship the collectibles. Last, you'll leave feedback for the buyer. In later chapters of this guide, each component of the selling process will be addressed in detail. Feedback, however, is such a unique eBay buying and selling feature that it should be discussed immediately.

Feedback

Feedback is the tool by which an eBay user's reputation is built and is a large part of an eBay seller's success. eBay users leave billions of feedback comments annually. There are three types of feedback: positive, neutral, and negative. Both parties in a transaction are encouraged to leave feedback about each other.

What you write in feedback becomes a permanent part of that user's record on eBay, so use caution and good judgment, especially before leaving negative comments. You cannot change or rename feedback once it's been posted.

An eBay user's feedback rating is reflected in a number in parentheses after his or her user ID. The feedback rating is calculated by giving one point for each positive comment, no points for a neutral comment, and subtracting one point for each negative comment. You should always check a user's profile for negative feedback, whether you're buying or selling.

If a user has hundreds of transactions on his or her record, don't let two negative remarks dissuade you from doing business with that person. Also, look at when the negative feedback was left—recently or a long time ago? Read the feedback and get a sense of whether it was justified or possibly retaliatory because the eBay member may have left negative feedback for that person. Many negative feedback comments are in retaliation for negative feedback the sellers have left about nonpaying bidders. So be sure to read all negative feedback comments and decide for yourself if they're valid.

If someone leaves you negative feedback, you will be able to respond to the comments—and you should so that others can see your side of the story. Keep the facts simple. "This is retaliatory feedback" or "Buyer refused refund" while remaining calm and professional. The sooner you leave feedback after completion of a transaction the better, but definitely do so within 90 days.

Seller Profiles

eBay Sellers are as diverse and unique as the collectors I discussed in the previous chapter. Each has their own specialty and runs their own type of business. The common denominator of the six sellers chosen for this guide, however, is that they are all well established and successful eBay sellers with nearly perfect feedback ratings. In the following chapters, these sellers will be sharing their experiences on selling collectibles on eBay.

Seller Profile 1

> *Seller name:* Beth Titus
> *Seller eBay screen name:* mel*molly
> *eBay member since:* 2000
> *Seller location:* New Hampshire
> *Seller's business:* Homebased, part time
> *Motivation to start business:* "I saw things at auctions, yard sales, and thrift shops that I thought I could resell. I like the thrill of buying something really cheap and making money at it."

Types of collectibles sold: All types, particularly modern collectibles from the 1960s and 1970s.

Reason for selling these collectibles: "I like collectibles from the '60s and '70s because they are relatively easy to find . . . . also, that's when I grew up, so the stuff is familiar and easier for me to recognize. The psychologists say that this is 'trying to get back your childhood.'"

Number of items sold annually: 500 to 600

Primary sources for these collectibles: Yard sales, auctions, thrift shops

Seller Profile 2

Seller's name: Jane Moen

Seller eBay screen name: Janee.

eBay member since: 1999

Seller location: Iowa

Seller's business: Homebased, started part time, but now full time, PowerSeller, About Me page, eBay Store

Motivation to start business: "Unhappy with present job and wanted a change in life."

Types of collectibles sold: Mostly glass, specialty is Fiesta-Ware.

Reason for selling these collectibles: "I chose Fiesta and glass . . . I have two sisters that also like Fiesta . . . so it has been kind of a family thing. I also love the bright colors and interesting shapes of Fiesta, and so many different styles and items. Also, glass is easy to ship if packed right."

SPOTLIGHT ON FIESTAWARE

In 1936, Fiesta Dinnerware was designed by Frederick Rhead for the Homer Laughlin China Company in Newell, West Virginia. The art deco design and bold, bright colors proved very popular. Original colors were red, yellow, cobalt, light green, and ivory, with turquoise being introduced the following year. The product was discontinued in 1973, but reissued again in 1986 with new colors to mark the 50th Anniversary.

In 2006, Fiestaware is now among the most collected china products in the world. When searching on eBay, I discovered it was wise to search for listings under both Fiestaware and Fiesta Ware. Using this method, I found more than 2,000 current listings and more than 4,500 completed listings of items in a rainbow of colors. The original colors had a lot of activity, but the newer items in hues like persimmon, sapphire, tangerine, and lilac were also very popular. I was particularly intrigued by several seemingly identical toasters that were being auctioned. Two were yellow and one was periwinkle blue. By the end of the auctions, all three had sold for between $50 and $60.

Number of items sold annually: 4,000

Primary sources for these collectibles: Estate auctions. "I go to one almost every week, and all the auctioneers in the area know me well . . . I go to auctions in a 100 mile radius."

Seller Profile 3

Seller name: Kathy Shaughnessy

Seller eBay screen name: bearfoottx

eBay member since: 1997

Seller location: Texas

Seller's business name: Bearfoot Gifts & Collectibles

Seller's business: Homebased, full time, PowerSeller, About Me page, eBay Store

Motivation to start business: "I saw the potential to make money selling collectibles."

Types of collectibles sold: Madame Alexander Dolls.

Reason for selling these collectibles: Madame Alexander Dolls are one of the oldest doll manufacturers. "There is a large collector base from which to purchase private collections, vintage as well as newer dolls."

Number of items sold annually: Approximately 4,800 dolls.

Primary sources for these collectibles: Private collectors and eBay

Seller Profile 4

Seller name: Larry and Cindy Brown

Seller eBay screen name: Granny4Xs

eBay member since: 1999

Seller location: Missouri

Seller's business name: Larry's Collectibles & Coke4u

Seller's business: Both home and commercial locations, started part time, now full time, PowerSeller, About Me page, eBay Store.

SPOTLIGHT ON MADAME ALEXANDER DOLLS

In 1923, Madame Alexander Doll Company was founded by Beatrice Alexander Behman and her sisters. These high-quality dolls were known for their exquisite outfits made of fine fabrics like satin and velvet, accompanied by beautiful accessories. Although there were relatively few faces on the Madame Alexander dolls, the individuality of each doll was in the costume. The dolls were marked with the Alexander name on the back of their heads.

In 2006, Gefinor Acquisition Partners currently owns the Madame Alexander line. They continue to produce high-quality dolls, but in greater quantities than in the past. A search of eBay showed 3,188 current listings and 7,268 completed listings for these dolls. There was a lot of activity on the 20-inch Cissy doll from the 1950s selling for $178.50 and a 1940s Black "Topsy" doll bringing in $917.77. Doll clothing was also in demand. In the completed listings I found two faux fur coats. One sold for $77, the other for $168.15.

Motivation to start business: "Thought an extra $100 week would help."

Types of collectibles sold: Mostly Coca Cola collectibles, also John Deere and other advertising collectibles.

Reason for selling these collectibles: "First, we enjoy collecting Coca Cola and advertising. Through the collecting, we realized there are lots of other collectors out there . . .

SPOTLIGHT ON COCA COLA

In 1894, Coca Cola was first bottled by Joseph Biedenharn in the hopes of reaching customers who did not live near his soda fountain. The enormously aggressive and successful advertising of this product since that time catapulted Coca Cola to worldwide prominence. The company used attractive people and clever slogans when advertising to help make this drink a symbol of the American way of life. Collectible items ranged from blotters to bookmarks, calendars to clocks, pocket mirrors to postcards, and even thermometers, all bearing the trademark logo.

In 2006, Coca Cola collectible items are alive and well on eBay. One search brought up more than 18,000 items with buyers bidding on many of them, especially older items like clocks and banners. One 15-foot 1950s rolled banner had ten bids with less than three hours left on the auction, and the price was $57.09. When I checked back, it had sold for $61.99. The huge volume of Coca Cola advertising items in all price ranges guarantees selection for buyers at all socioeconomic levels.

Coca Cola is one, if not the top advertising collectible. . . . The new items are easy for anyone to collect and lots of fun, with lots of new things coming out every year."

Number of items sold annually: 2400+

Primary sources for these collectibles: "We purchase directly from the manufacturers mostly."

Seller Profile 5

Seller name: Sam Buchanan

Seller eBay screen name: 3-oldstuff-3

eBay member since: 2002

Seller location: California

Seller's business name: 3-oldstuff-3

Seller's business: Part-time, in addition to being a real estate broker, runs an eBay business from a spare commercial office.

Motivation to start business: "I have always had old cars and I want another. My wife said to get rid of something. I collect many things: watches, toy cars, books, etc."

Types of collectibles sold: Postcards and old photos.

Reason for selling these collectibles: "I started collecting postcards 30 years ago and decided to sell them to buy an antique car which I bought on eBay!"

Number of items sold annually: 5,000

Primary sources for these collectibles: "My collection—and I go to estate sales."

Seller Profile 6

Seller name: Scott Gaynor

Seller eBay screen name: Scgaynor

eBay member since: 1997

Seller location: Massachusetts

Seller's business name: Scgaynor Auctions

Seller's business: Commercial, but not open for retail, full time, PowerSeller, About Me page, eBay Store

Motivation to start business: "I had been out of college for about two years and started by selling odds and ends that were sitting around my apartment and developed a following pretty quick for sports memorabilia. As eBay got bigger, so did my customer base which allowed me to sell bigger and better items."

Types of collectibles sold: Vintage Sports Memorabilia, Autographs, Historical Documents, Rock n Roll Memorabilia, Hollywood Memorabilia, Vintage collectibles of all types.

Reason for selling these collectibles: "It was my hobby growing up and I decided to turn it into a business."

Number of items sold annually: "We sell 200 to 300 lots per week. A lot may be one piece or thousands of pieces."

Primary sources for these collectibles: "We take all of our materials on consignment. We charge between 15 and 20 percent (by far the lowest rates in the business) and accept lots valued at $100 or more."

Many Kinds of eBay Sellers

As you can see from the profiles above, there is a wide range of collectible sellers on eBay. From small, homebased, part-time operations to large, commercial, full-time endeavors, these six eBay sellers have all found success. It doesn't matter where in the country they live or what their collectible interests are, eBay offers them all the perfect place to market their merchandise on the internet.

Own What
They Want

As an eBay seller, one of your first concerns is choosing what collectible items you want to sell. Maybe, like Sam Buchanan, you have already acquired an antique postcard collection and are now willing to part with some of it. Or maybe, like Beth Titus, you constantly spot things from the 1960s and 1970s at tag sales and auctions that you know you can sell for a profit. Of course, you may also have just inherited three boxes of Fenton "Carnival" glassware from a relative and you're really not interested in keeping them all. The bottom line is that the collectibles you sell have to be items you already own or ones you can easily acquire.

SPOTLIGHT ON FENTON GLASS

In 1907, the Fenton Art Glass Company of West Virginia introduced "iridescent" glass, currently know as "Carnival" glass. This inexpensively produced glass was made by spraying or daubing metallic salts onto pressed colored glass. Carnival glass is among the most popular of glass collectibles as it comes in a variety of appealing colors, shapes, and patterns. Marigold is one of the most common base colors, but Fenton launched a red product in 1920. Often called the "poor man's Tiffany," Carnival glass was produced through the 1920s.

In 2006, Fenton is the largest manufacturer of handmade colored glass in the United States, employing 500 skilled glassworkers and decorators. An eBay search showed 783 current listings for their Carnival glass and 1,641 completed listings. There were a several "Thistle" bowls in a variety of colors listed, all with a number of bids on them. When I checked back, a green one had sold for $39 and a blue one drew a bid of $66.

Demand

To be successful as a seller, you have to be sure that there is a demand for the collectibles you want to sell. It would be devastating if you bought hundreds or thousands of porcelain piggy banks and then no one wanted them. You certainly wouldn't be in business very long. It is important to determine that the collectibles you want to sell have a fighting chance in the eBay marketplace. To do this, you have to do your homework and become as much of an expert as possible regarding your specific collectibles.

Becoming an Expert

There are a number of ways to gain knowledge about your particular collectibles. You need to immerse yourself in the subject by reading books and periodicals, consulting price guides, browsing informational web sites, and networking with other collectors. Knowledge is power and you want as much as possible so you can use it to your best advantage.

Books, Periodicals, and Price Guides

Your local library or bookstore should have general books and price guides on collectibles as well as titles on specific collectible items. Libraries may also carry periodicals, or magazines, that relate to collectibles. For additional resources, check online bookstores such as Amazon.com or Barnesand Noble.com.

Informational Web Sites

The internet is a wide and wonderful place. Use a search engine such as Google.com to

The Seller Says . . .

Kathy says, "Specialize in one product and become an expert on your product."

The Seller Says...

Scott says, "Google is a tool that we could not do without, the information available is incredible."

help locate sites that pertain to your collectibles. And don't forget to use eBay as a resource. Searching the completed listings for your items can provide a wealth of knowledge.

Networking

It never hurts to talk to people. Collectors are generally friendly folk and are willing to share their knowledge. Consider joining a club that specializes in your type of collectible. Whether you collect Disneyana or ephemera, there is probably a club or an association you can join. Some send out newsletters, others have meetings or conventions. Use Google or another search engine to help you find the ones that relate to your particular collectibles.

TIP

Approach information you find on the internet with caution. Not everyone is as knowledgeable as they think they are. A good strategy when collecting information about the items you wish to sell is to read and digest as much as possible until you feel comfortable with the subject.

Finding Inventory

Collectors buy things that they love. It is your job, as a seller of collectibles, to identify and find these items so they can be purchased by the collectors seeking them. Once you've decided which collectibles you want to sell, you have a number of ways to obtain an inventory. You might start by selling things

SPOTLIGHT ON DISNEYANA

In 1928, the cartoon, Steamboat Willie, opened to rave reviews at the Colony Theater in New York. It made Mickey Mouse a star! Originally, Walt Disney himself provided the voice for this beloved character, who would go on to appear in over 120 different cartoons. Soon Mickey's likeness could be found on everything from dolls to toothbrushes, lunch boxes to pajamas.

In 2006, Disneyana is probably one of the broadest collectible categories. The familiar characters can be found on toys, dolls, trading cards, trading pins, puzzles, plush toys, clothing, figurines, watches, and much more. In the hundreds of current and completed eBay listings, I found everything from older Snow White items to recent Incredibles paraphernalia. Many small items like patches and mugs were not getting a lot of activity, but more interesting listings like the one for 30 Disney pins (many limited edition) sold for $75.98.

from your own collections. Then you could hit up your family and friends for merchandise. After that, however, you must find new ways to replenish your inventory. Places to investigate include garage sales, flea markets, thrift stores, antique shows, estate sales, gift stores, and auctions, both live and online. A solid inventory is essential to your success on eBay.

Garage Sales

People periodically clean out their homes and sell the items at a garage/yard sale. Often, they get rid of great things just because they no longer have a use for it. Usually, the price is pretty cheap. Many times, the owner may have no idea of the true value of an item. Thankfully, it is not your place to tell them. Get to yard sales early and look for some great bargains.

Flea Markets

Flea markets offer a larger number of sellers and a greater amount of merchandise than a garage sale. Once again, it is potluck—you never know if you'll find a number of wonderful collectibles, or nothing at all.

Thrift Stores

Many charitable organizations run thrift stores where people can drop off unwanted items. These things include clothing, books, furniture, or even collectibles. It never hurts to stop in regularly to see what is available.

Antique Shows

The sellers at antique shows are likely to be more knowledgeable than someone at a garage sale, and their prices are bound to be higher. However, it is still possible to find collectibles to resell. Even if you don't pick up inventory at one of these shows, you might meet other people interested in the same thing and gain more insight into your collectibles.

Estate Sales

If the estate sale is run by an estate-liquidation company, you can expect higher prices than if it is run by family members. These companies know what they are doing and are familiar with the type of merchandise they are selling. They are not going to give it away. You may, however, be able to get a better deal at the end of the sale when they are ready to discount in order to sell as much as possible.

Gift Stores

Many gift stores sell new collectibles. Watch for their sales and pick up items you can resell on eBay. If a store in your area decides to go out of business, this might be the perfect opportunity for you to pick up a large amount of inventory at a deep discount. If you offer to take all of their inventory, the owner may give you a very good price.

Live Auctions

Many communities hold live auctions on a regular basis. Usually, you can preview the materials ahead of time so that you can inspect the merchandise and determine what items you want to bid on. Some auctions have online viewing several days in advance, others offer this opportunity only a few hours before the auction begins. Although these auctions can be hit or miss in terms of finding inventory, that is all part of the fun of going to them. You never know what you might find.

Online Auctions

Many eBay sellers of collectibles find items to resell right on eBay. They bid and win pieces at a reasonable price and later sell them for much more. Using a search engine such as Google will also allow you to find other online auction sites that might be of interest.

Storage Unit Buyouts

Self-storage unit owners in some areas hold auctions on the contents of units where the rent has not been paid. These auctions are advertised in the newspaper. Although you can't usually preview what you are bidding on, you could score big if you're willing to take the risk.

How Much to Spend

Be cautious when you first start buying inventory to sell on eBay. In an ideal situation, you hope to buy an item for a small amount of money, and then sell it for a great deal more. If you've done the homework on your collectibles, it will be much easier to spot an underpriced object and know when you are getting a real deal. You can be more confident about spending your money if you know what the item has sold for recently on eBay.

Spending Mistakes

All sellers make purchasing mistakes. Beware of "auction fever" where you keep bidding past the top price you had planned to pay. Stop yourself when you reach your predetermined limit. If someone is willing to pay more than you for an item, let them have it. You don't want to pay so much for something that you can't earn your money back when you try to resell it.

Always preview items that you are considering buying. Make sure you get a close look so you can determine the condition of the item. Never bid on a whim if you haven't checked out the merchandise. You could be disappointed with your purchase.

On the other hand, if you see an item you are confident is a good deal, don't hesitate too long in deciding whether to buy it. Someone else may snatch it up in the meantime. Prepare yourself to make mistakes. Don't beat yourself up over them when you do. Learning from both the good and bad experiences is part of the business.

As an example, let's consider the following situation. At a family-run estate sale in a neighboring town, you see a box full of old baseballs stuffed under a table. When you look closer, you realize that each one of them has a signature on it. If you regularly sell Sports Memorabilia, you might know immediately if this is a gold mine but, unfortunately, your collectible specialty is glass. In this case, you would be wise to

SPOTLIGHT ON SIGNED BASEBALLS

In 1914, the celebrity of Babe Ruth helped make collecting signed baseballs a popular American pastime. Players were accessible to the fans at this time, and balls could easily be autographed. Whether the baseball received a single signature, or those of the whole team, these keepsakes were treasured by the fans that idolized both the game and its players. Collecting signed baseballs was an emotional investment rather than a financial one.

In 2006, the baseballs for sale on eBay today are signed not only by baseball players but by NASCAR drivers, country singers, politicians, actors, television personalities, and sports stars from many different sports. According to the completed listings on eBay, there seems to be a market for most of them. A baseball signed by Sonny Barger, founder of Hells Angels Motorcycle Club, just sold for $227.50. A smart eBay Seller will use an authentication service to obtain a Certificate of Authenticity on any autograph before they list it.

only pay as much money as you are willing to lose. You won't know if you've made a good or bad decision until you've researched the baseballs to see if the signatures are authentic. You can't be an expert on everything but, over time, you will probably develop a sense of quality items versus junk. As you hunt for your own specialty items, you are bound to run across other collectibles that you might be able to sell. Trust your instincts but, unless you are absolutely positive of their value, do not lay out a huge amount of cash. By keeping abreast of the different eBay collectible categories, you'll be better able to spot a new opportunity when it presents itself.

Main Collectible eBay Categories

As of this writing, the following are the main categories that eBay lists for collectibles. However, a message sent to all eBay users on January 18, 2006, announced a new category structure for later in the spring. This list will likely expand and change:

- Advertising
- Animals
- Animation Art, Characters
- Arcade, Jukeboxes and Pinball
- Autographs
- Banks, Registers and Vending
- Barware
- Bottles and Insulators
- Breweriana, Beer
- Casino
- Clocks
- Comics
- Cultures, Ethnicities
- Decorative Collectibles
- Disneyana

- Fantasy, Mythical, and Magic
- Furniture, Appliances, and Fans
- Historical Memorabilia
- Holiday, Seasonal
- Housewares and Kitchenware
- Knives, Swords, and Blades
- Lamps, Lighting
- Linens, Fabric, and Textile
- Metalware
- Militaria
- Pens and Writing Instruments
- Pez, Keychains, Promo Glasses
- Photographic Images

- Pinbacks, Nodders, Lunchboxes
- Postcards and Paper
- Radio, Phonograph, TV, Phone
- Religions, Spirituality
- Rocks, Fossils, Minerals
- Science Fiction
- Science, Medical
- Tobacciana
- Tools, Hardware, and Locks
- Trading Cards
- Transportation
- Vanity, Perfume, and Shaving
- Vintage Sewing
- Wholesale Lots

CHAPTER 4

To Auction
or Not

*T*O PUT A COLLECTIBLE UP FOR AUCTION ON EBAY IS NOT complicated or difficult; however, it's not quite as simple as it sounds. The online auction world is not a one-size-fits-all proposition. As you're getting started, you may want to do some experimenting with the different types of eBay auctions to see how they work and what might be best for you and your particular products.

Traditional Auctions

Traditional auctions are the backbone of eBay. They run for 1, 3, 5, 7, or 10 days. The auction begins with an opening bid and when the

> ### The Seller Says...
>
> Kathy says, "I prefer an auction for the potential of a higher selling price."

time is up, the highest bidder is the winner. This is a very easy process; however, depending on your business strategy and the type of product you are selling, you may want to think about using other types of auction formats.

Reserve Price Auction

Auctions that have a hidden minimum price are known as reserve price auctions. The reserve price is the lowest amount the seller is willing to accept for the item. Buyers are not shown what the reserve price is; they only see that there is a reserve price, and whether or not it has been met. If the reserve price is not met at the end of the auction, the seller is not obligated to sell the item. To win the auction, a bidder must meet or exceed the reserve price and have the highest bid.

In a reserve price auction, bids are made as usual, but bidders receive a notice if their bid does not meet the reserve price. Once the reserve is met, the item will sell to the highest bidder when the auction closes. See how reserve pricing affected a recent Hummel figurine sale in the Spotlight on Hummel/Goebel.

Buy It Now (BIN)

Buy It Now (BIN) is a feature you can add to a traditional auction format that gives bidders the option to bid on your

SPOTLIGHT ON HUMMEL/GOEBEL

In 1935, Hummel handpainted figurines were first produced by the German company W. Goebel. They were inspired by paintings done by Sister M. I. Hummel, a nun in Nazi Germany. Although, she died an early death in 1946, her spirit continued to live on in the innocence and beauty portrayed in the children and religious figures that appeared on plates, bells, candle holders, bookends, holy water fonts, ornaments, music boxes, ashtrays, lamps, and clocks.

In 2006, an eBay search of Hummels shows that these figurines are still very popular with nearly 12,000 auctions completed and 3,499 items currently listed. As I scanned through the items, most had multiple bids on them, and the average price was running in the $40 to $80 range with only minutes left on each auction. The hottest item was a 9-inch MIB Flower Madonna figurine. When I checked back after the auction had ended, there had been 16 bidders and the price had risen to $282. Unfortunately for the high bidder, the seller had set a reserve price and it wasn't reached. The seller kept their Madonna.

product or to buy it immediately. With BIN, you set the price you're willing to sell for, and bidders can either place a bid for less than that amount (but at or above your starting price) or win the auction instantly by paying the BIN amount. When a bidder agrees to the BIN price, the auction

TIP

If you have a collectible that is highly sought after, the BIN option might be a good one for you. Educated buyers may avoid any competition by purchasing the item immediately. Be sure you have researched previously sold items so you can set a fair price.

ends. If someone places a bid below the BIN price, the BIN option disappears.

Fixed-Price Listings

Technically, a fixed-price listing is not an auction because there is no bidding, but those listings show up in auction search results. This format allows users to buy and sell items immediately at a set price, with no bidding or waiting. You can sell more than one of an item in a fixed-price listing, which saves you time and money in listing fees.

Private Auctions

In most auction formats, anyone looking at the item can see the user IDs of the people who are bidding on it. With the private auction format, however, the bidders' user IDs are not seen on the item or bidding history screens. When the auction is over, only the seller and winning bidder are notified via e-mail.

This format is useful when you believe your prospective bidders may not want their identities disclosed to the general public. Well-known collectors often prefer private auctions. A common use of this format is when the knowledge that a certain collector is bidding on an item would greatly increase the interest in the auction. Private auctions are also appropriate for items not intended for mass viewing, such as adult material.

Dutch Auctions

When a seller offers two or more identical items for sale in the same auction, it's known as a Dutch (or multiple item) auction, where you sell large quantities of a single item with just one listing.

When you post a Dutch auction, you decide on the minimum bid amount you're willing to accept and list that along with the total number of identical items you have available. Bidders specify the quantity they're interested in and the highest price they're willing to pay per item.

What makes Dutch auctions interesting—and complicated— is that all winning bidders pay the same price per item, which is the lowest successful bid. Most commonly, all buyers pay the starting price. But if there are more bids than items, the items will go to the earliest successful bids at the close of the auction. Bidders may bid on any quantity but have the right to refuse partial quantities.

Bidders in Dutch auctions do not receive outbid notices from eBay, nor can they use eBay's proxy bidding system (which allows a bidder to enter a hidden maximum bid), so they must actively monitor the auction and rebid if necessary.

The most important things to keep in mind when using the Dutch auction format are that the items in a single Dutch auction must be absolutely identical, and the auction itself must be listed in the appropriate category.

Don't be tempted to try something known as "Dutch avoidance"—that is, listing a single item and offering additional identical items for sale in the item description—the practice is dishonest and against eBay policy. Listings that violate this guideline will be terminated by eBay.

Live Auctions

This particular type of auction is of more interest to an online buyer than a seller, but it's something you should know about. eBay's live auctions feature allows you to bid real time on auctions that are happening on the floor of offline auction events. You can place absentee bids, bid against the floor, or just watch the auction—all from the convenience of your home or office. For more information, go to www.ebayliveauctions.com.

Restricted-Access Auctions

This category makes it easy for buyers and sellers to find or avoid adult-only merchandise. To sell, view, and bid on adult-only items, users must have a credit card on file with eBay. Items listed in the adult-only category are not included on eBay's New Items page or the Hot Items section, nor are they

---

SPOTLIGHT ON DC COMICS

In 1938, DC Comics, one of the oldest comic companies introduced Superman, followed shortly by Batman. These characters were wildly popular and paved the way for many other superhero characters like The Flash, Green Lantern, and Wonder Woman. Over time these characters moved into other media including radio, television, and film. The licensed characters also began to appear on clothing, toys, and other products.

In 2006, no matter what your budget, you can find plenty of DC Comics on eBay. When I searched, there were 10,159 current listings and 23,142 completed listings. Prices ranged from around $1 to thousands and thousands of dollars. Many large lots were being sold, but the higher priced individual comics were mainly sold via live auction. The most expensive one sold was Action Comics number one, which topped out at $60,000!

---

available by any title search. Failure to list an adult-only item in the correct area could result in a suspension of your eBay account.

eBay's policies stipulate that all users must abide by all applicable regulations regarding the sale and distribution of adult materials, and any violation of the law is also a violation of eBay's user agreement, and will be treated accordingly.

Want It Now

This is a type of classified ads section where buyers can post requests for specific items and sellers are able to respond with matching eBay listings. This free service enables sellers to expand their market by actively looking for buyers for items they have on hand. You can search by category or keywords. You can also save your searches to be used again and elect to receive alerts on corresponding Want It Now (WIN) requests. Once you've determined that you have a matching item, you can then send an e-mail to the buyer through eBay with a link to your listing. One out of two WIN bids results in a successful transaction.

When I browsed through the collectibles WIN listings, people were looking for things like Three Stooges figurines, amber Coke bottles, White Sox bobbleheads, and a *Saturday Evening Post* from 1911. Also, a number of people were looking for replacement Longaberger parts for their basket collections.

Best Offer

As a seller, you can choose to allow prospective buyers to make an offer on your listing; however, these auctions need to be set up as a fixed-price format. Many buyers search specifically for auctions that have a Submit Best Offer feature, so this can be an additional marketing tool. Once the offer has been made, you and the buyer can start your negotiations. Best offers are binding and all messages relating to the transaction

SPOTLIGHT ON LONGABERGER

In 1973, the Longaberger Company was founded in Ohio by Dave Longaberger, whose grandfather had shown him the fine art of making handmade baskets. Each basket was individually crafted and signed on the bottom by its creator. Dave believed that baskets were not only useful, but beautiful, and consumers would appreciate quality items. The brisk sale of Longaberger baskets proved that he was right.

In 2006, through direct sales marketing, rather than retail outlets, this family-owned company has grown to over 5,000 employees and produces not only baskets, but fabric accessories, pottery, wrought iron, and specialty foods. An eBay search showed more than 10,000 current and 23,803 completed listings, with lots of activity on most of them. One interesting thing I noted was that, in the current auctions, the pre-1990 baskets did not have as many bidders as those produced more recently.

must be conducted through eBay and not violate any trading policies. Buyers are only allowed to make one offer per listing, so if you decline a bid, the buyer cannot come back and try to haggle with you. This is to encourage people to seriously make their best offer from the onset. You will receive an e-mail notifying you when a Best Offer has been made and you have

48 hours to respond before the offer expires. So check your messages often.

eBay Stores

Along with putting merchandise up for auction on eBay, you may want to consider opening an eBay store, which allows you to sell your fixed price and auction items from a unique destination on eBay. eBay stores make it easy to cross-sell your inventory and build repeat business. More information on eBay stores is provided in Chapter 9.

eBay Express

On January 18, 2006, eBay announced a new specialty site called eBay Express. It will launch in the spring of 2006 and will provide buyers with a way to purchase things right away. Many eBay sellers can benefit from this site as they will not have to list their inventory twice and payment will be made immediately. Qualified Store and Fixed Price listings will appear on both eBay.com and eBay Express. Sellers must have a positive track record, 98 percent feedback rating, and a feedback score of at least 100 to participate. They must also accept PayPal. More details will be made available on eBay in the coming months, so keep checking the web site.

CHAPTER 5

Proper
Pricing

YOU NEED TO HAVE A SERIOUS PRICING STRATEGY WHEN IT comes to pricing the collectibles you want to sell. You want to make the most money for the least investment. Unfortunately, this can be tricky when you are auctioning items rather than selling them at a fixed price. When setting prices for eBay auctions, you need to consider the fees you have to pay at each price level and the known value of the collectibles.

eBay Fees

The fees that eBay charges are set, but they do change occasionally. In fact, an eBay General Announcement has been made that states as of February 22, 2006, there will be basic fee changes. The new Insertion Fees are listed in Table 5.1 and Final Value Fee schedules are listed in Table 5.2.

TABLE 5.1
Insertion Fees

Starting or Reserve Price	Insertion Fee
$.01–$.99	$.20
$1.00–$9.99	$.35
$10.00–$24.99	$.60
$25.00–$49.99	$1.20
$50.00–$199.99	$2.40
$200.00–$499.99	$3.60
$500.00 or more	$4.80

Value

As discussed in Chapter 3, the value of your items requires some research. You should consult books, periodicals, web sites (including eBay), and specific organizations that deal

TABLE 5.2
Final Value Fees

Closing Price Item not Sold	Final Value Fee No Fee
$.01–$25.00	5.25% of the closing value.
$25.01–$1,000.00	5.25% of the initial $25.00 plus 3% of the remaining closing value balance.
Over $1,000.01	5.25% of the initial $25.00 plus 3% of the initial $25.00–$1,000.00 plus 1.5% of the remaining closing value.

with your collectibles. You must have a good idea of what that collectible is worth before you put it up for sale.

Helpful eBay Research Tools

eBay offers two research tools that can help you determine prices for your listings. They are the Completed Listings search and Market Research.

A WORD ABOUT PRICE GUIDES

Collectible price guides like Kovels, Millers, and Schroeders are issued annually. These can be helpful in determining an item's value, but they are certainly not the only source you should use when fixing a collectible's price. Price guides are a great tool to have in your car if you are visiting flea markets, garage sales, or estate sales. If you spot something you think might be valuable, you can easily refer to the book and then make an educated decision on your purchase. Many price guides contain numerous color photographs to assist you.

Completed Listings Search

The Completed Listings Search is available free to any eBay User. It contains all the items that have closed in the last two weeks. You can view the starting and ending prices on these listings, as well as all the other listing information. With careful study, you can see what price and listing strategies work, and then create your own listings accordingly.

I had to question the logic of the seller from South Carolina who was trying to sell Waterman pens recently on eBay. They had five identical listings with a starting bid on each one of $17.95. Only two of them sold, and only for the starting price. At the exact same time, this seller had four other

Waterman listings where he was trying to sell different pens in suites of two and four. These had starting bids of $29.95 and $59.95. None of them sold. This Waterman seller might

SPOTLIGHT ON WATERMAN PENS

In 1900, a Waterman pen won the Medal of Excellence at the Paris World Exposition. Louis E. Waterman's fountain pens were elegant, yet affordable and reliable. Some had intricate designs while others were more plain, but had gold bands. These beautiful, high-quality productions remained popular through World War I and up to the Depression, at which time people could no longer afford them. When the economy improved, the new ballpoint pen gained popularity, and the fountain pen's marketability faded. The American branch of Waterman Pen closed in 1958.

In 2006, many collectors still appreciate the beauty and design of the Waterman pens. A search on eBay pulls up 740 current listings and 1,671 completed listings for these items. Healthy bidding was occurring on most of the current items but, certainly, the older pens were receiving more attention than the later models. One vintage English Waterman 515 Fountain Pen from 1946 sold for almost $70, while another vintage Waterman Ideal Orange and Black Fountain Pen was topping out at $160.25.

want to reconsider his listing strategies so as not to create such a glut on the market.

Market Research

Market Research is a new tool offered by eBay where you can access up to 90 days of eBay historical completed items data. If your budget allows for this paid service, you can have access to average starting prices, average sold prices, top searches by category, and graphs with buying and selling trends.

Pricing an Auction

All auction pricing is dynamic and fluid. What works one day may not work the next. Not every transaction will be profitable but, if you are careful in your pricing strategies, you should be able to keep losses to a minimum.

The Seller Says . . .

Jane says, "I spend a lot of time searching through ended auctions on eBay. Books are not much help, because what a book says they are worth and what they sell for on eBay are two different things."

Starting Bid

For every auction, you will need to enter a starting price. This is the price at which the bidding will begin. When you set this price, keep in mind that a low starting price tends to attract bidders, whereas a

---

TIP

Watch the point at which the listing fees go up. These fees look small, but they can really add up if you're not careful. Each time you start your item at $.99 rather than $1.00, you will save yourself $.15.

---

high starting price discourages them. Do not set your starting bid at the current market value of your collectible. The odds are it won't sell and you'll still have to pay eBay the listing fee. Things to consider that might affect your starting price are how much you paid for the item, how much similar pieces have sold for on eBay, and how emotionally attached you are to it.

Reserve Price

Auctions that have a hidden minimum price are known as reserve price auctions. Sellers see reserve pricing as a way to protect their investment without revealing up front how much they want to get for the item. You can also lose customers, as many bidders avoid reserve auctions because they

The Seller Says . . .

Beth says, "If I have something that I want to start at a higher starting price than $9.99, I try to wait until eBay offers the discount listing days."

can't tell what the lowest winning bid needs to be, and they don't want to waste their time bidding on an item that may have a high reserve figure. You pay an extra cost for the "insurance" built into a reserve price auction, but it is refunded if your item sells.

Buy It Now (BIN)

> ### The Seller Says...
>
> Jane says, "I sell different ways. Lesser priced items, I take a chance on and start them low. I don't use Buy It Now much, just in my store. On things that are higher priced, I like to start low and use a reserve."

This feature gives bidders the option to either bid on your product or to buy it immediately. A good pricing strategy used by many sellers is to start the bidding at the absolute minimum you will accept for the

> ### The Seller Says...
>
> Cindy says, "I do a Buy It Now on over 99 percent of our auctions. I start with the price the item is worth and set the Buy It Now at or close to the starting price."

item, then set the BIN amount close to full retail. If you get anything in between, you've made a profit and the customer is happy with their bargain. As with a reserve price, there is an additional eBay fee.

Many buyers take advantage of the Buy It Now feature. One Lladro lover snatched up a 7-by-9½-inch figurine of a family cuddling together called "A Priceless Moment" for $475. The seller claimed the 2005 retail value was $650. One can only assume that the buyer thought they were getting a bargain.

Fixed-Price Listing

A fixed-price listing is exactly what it says it is. You, as the seller, decide how much you want for your collectible, then list it. If someone is willing to pay what you ask, then you have a sale. A fixed-price listing is not considered an auction because there is no bidding involved.

The Seller Says...

Beth says, "I use Buy It Now when there are quite a few of the same item I'm listing, all of which are around the same price. I price it near the top of the selling average."

TIP

When pricing, keep in mind that the total price someone has to pay is their winning bid, or your fixed price, plus the shipping costs.

SPOTLIGHT ON LLADRO CERAMICS

In 1955, the first Lladro retail shop opened in Velencia, Spain. The company, founded by three brothers, specialized in beautifully crafted porcelain figurines with an elongated design. Growth was steady, especially in the 1960s when their factory workshop in Tabernas was enlarged seven times and they began exporting to other countries. Artists used manual techniques in addition to molds, so each of the charming figurines produced was unique.

In 2006, Lladro now has over 2,000 employees and retail stores in over 120 countries. Some figures are retired annually and pieces from the 1950s are rare. A search on eBay showed 487 current listings and 1,310 completed listings. There were numerous bids on many of these figurines, and it is common to see final sale prices over $100. One completed auction for two soccer players on a wooden stand had 20 bids and sold for $480.59, even though the soccer ball had been glued back on!

CHAPTER 6

Winning
Listings

*T*HERE'S A LOGICAL SEQUENCE TO GETTING AN AUCTION
posted on eBay. Learn how to do it manually
before you graduate to automated systems. Start
by choosing your listing type from the options we've discussed. If
you're unsure, consider what successful sellers have used for similar products.

Determine Your Starting Price

This is the lowest price you're willing to accept for your item (unless
you have specified a reserve price), and this is the amount at which
bidding starts. Be reasonable when calculating this figure. Certainly

you want to make a profit on what you sell, but sellers have found that setting the starting price too high often discourages bidding. A lower starting amount may attract a flurry of initial bidders who will quickly drive the price up. If you are using a fixed price format, you'll enter a Buy It Now price.

Write Your Title

eBay allows 55 characters (letters and spaces) for your listing's title, so make each one count. Your title must make a prospective bidder want to learn more about your auction. It helps if your headline is clever and catchy, but above all, it must be accurate and factual. Misleading titles are against eBay policy and could result in eBay ending your auction early. Though you might see them often, devices such as "L@@K" and excessive exclamation points don't attract additional bidders—but they do brand you as an amateur. Use all caps sparingly and only to make certain words stand out.

Your title needs to include the key words that someone who is looking for your item might conduct a search for. If you have room, include a related word so your listing will come up in more searches. Be creative in the language you use in your titles. Think of everything your item relates to, and figure out how you might be able to get as many of those words as possible into your title. Your title should also indicate why your listing is special. If you are selling a brand-name item, include the brand in the title. If the item is clothing or something that comes in different sizes, indicate the size.

Sample Title
Art Deco 1927 Cassandre Etoile du Nord Poster No Repro

Write Your Description

Investing time in writing a good description will pay off in the price you receive. Your description should include the name of the item, what the item is made of, when and where it was made, who made it (company, artist, designer, author, etc.), what condition it's in, weight, size, and/or dimensions, notable features or markings, and any special background or history.

Sample Description
Original 1927 Art Deco Poster entitled "Etoile du Nord" by the famous Adolphe Mouron Cassandre. This poster measures 24 x 36 inches and is in good condition with some repaired tears and minor fading. It has been part of a framed collection at our local public library, and has been kept out of direct sunlight. Shipping is $8 if you want it sent unframed. Actual shipping charges will be determined if you want it shipped in the frame. Insurance is required in either case. We accept checks, money orders, or PayPal. We ship worldwide. Sorry, but we do not accept returns.

Everything in your description should be true and accurate. If an item is damaged or missing parts, don't say something vague such as "easily restored." If possible, identify exactly what needs to be replaced or suggest the buyer purchase the

SPOTLIGHT ON ART DECO POSTERS

In 1935, Art Deco artist Adolphe Mouron Cassandre created the striking poster image of the French ship *Normandie*. Using geometric designs, bold colors, and stylized form, his posters, and those of other artists of the time, were used to advertise many things including sports, food, clothing, travel, cars, and liquor. As photo-offset printing became more widely used, reproductions could be easily made.

In 2006, reproductions of Art Deco posters are readily available both online and offline for a reasonable price. The original posters, however, are much harder to come by. A search of eBay confirmed that although there were 433 current listings, most of them were reproductions without much activity. The same held true for the 1,122 completed auctions. When I focused specifically on Cassandre's work, two interesting current listings appeared. One was a new listing for a 1935 Italian travel poster that was not a reproduction. This original poster had a starting bid of $250 that had already been taken. When I checked back a few days later, the price was up to $400 but the reserve had not yet been met. A week or so later, this poster's auction ended and it had sold for $1,405 (and the reserve was met). The other interesting item was a 1937 copy of *Fortune* magazine that contained four of Cassandre's original posters. It ended up selling for $55.32.

item to be used as parts for another piece. You might also add a personal touch to your description; many sellers have found that doing so can increase bids and sales. For example, specifically say what you like about the item, who it would

appeal to and why, or how it could be used. If you know an interesting story about the item, share it. If the item is not in perfect condition, be honest. Describe any scratches, chips, stains, and other imperfections.

Avoid keyword spamming, which is including words in your description that are not actually related to your item just because you think buyers would find those words appealing and because they are words a search would pick up. This is against eBay's listing policies. However, do use as many legitimate search words and phrases in your description as possible to be sure your item will come up when bidders are searching.

You can also use your description to add details about shipping costs, payment terms, and any other details you think may be of interest to a bidder.

Even if you plan to charge actual shipping, it's always a good idea to include at least an estimate of the shipping costs so bidders aren't surprised when the auction is over. Also, let bidders know if there are any restrictions on where you will ship, such as U.S. only, U.S. and Canada only, or to certain

COMMON COLLECTIBLE CONDITION PROBLEMS

Collectibles are prone to damage, and all flaws must be reported in your auction listings. Here are some common problems you should look for before you try to sell your items.

Crazing: tiny cracks on the surface or glaze

Crack: a flaw caused by age

Chip: a small piece broken off

Stains: a soiled or discolored spot

Scratch: a scrape or mark

Cloudiness: to make unclear

Tear: damage from being torn

Crease: a line, mark, or ridge made by folding

Discoloration: to alter the color

Previous repair: use black light to find spots

international locations. eBay has a shipping calculator that you can insert in your auctions to allow the buyer to determine how much it will cost to send that specific item to their address via United States Postal Service (USPS) or United

Parcel Service (UPS). When you're finished, proofread and spell check, and then proofread again.

Choose the Right Category

Browse eBay and find items that are similar to what you want to sell, and see what categories they're listed in. Check completed auctions to see what the final sale price was, and look for trends that would indicate that listing an item in one particular category gets better results than another. Listing in the wrong category is a big mistake.

> **The Seller Says . . .**
>
> Beth says, "I don't think it looks professional to put whiny comments in your listings . . . like 'don't bid if you're not going to pay' or 'the post office loses too many things.'"

Make Your Pictures Worth More than 1,000 Words

A photo, indicated by a camera icon in your listing, will make a tremendous difference in the success of your auctions. Quality photos not only let bidders see what your product really looks like, but they also say that you're a serious, professional eBay seller.

Here are some tips to produce quality photos:

- Create a photo area in your home or shop with good lighting and a background screen for an uncluttered background.

- Consider developing a photo background with a distinctive color, pattern, logo, or company name that helps brand your business.

- If appropriate, showcase your item with accessories to display it to its best advantage. Be sure to indicate whether those accessories are included in the auction, are available separately, or are not for sale.

- If you sell clothing or jewelry, invest in used mannequins to properly display them. A box draped with a piece of plain fabric works as a display pedestal.

- Maintain a database of pictures so it's easy to pull up images for listings when you are selling items you've sold before.

- Invest in a quality digital camera.

- If you have a scanner, you can use print film and then scan your photos.

Once you have the pictures uploaded to your computer, you can then use a program or software to adjust and enhance your images.

Listing Strategies

Your listing strategies will depend on your personal schedule and the buying habits of those collectors you are trying to attract. It will probably take some trial and error to see which times of the day and which days of the week are most successful for listing and completing your auctions. Some sellers always end their auctions on Sundays, whereas others avoid the weekends at all costs. Over time you will discover what listing strategies work best for you. In the meantime, there are a couple of things you can do that might make a big difference in the success of your collectible listing.

Check current auctions to see if there are similar collectible items already listed. If there are, see what they are priced at and watch the auctions until they end. Wait to list your collectible until after the other auctions are complete. You will know what the final selling price was, and that item will no longer be your competition.

Also look at the completed auctions to see when similar items started and ended. Check to see if they received a good sale price. If there were no buyers, you might want to wait a while before listing your item.

There may be obvious reasons some of the items you find in the completed auctions didn't sell. For one thing, their starting price may have been too high. Another possible reason is that their timing was off for the particular item they were trying to sell. For example, when I searched the completed auctions for Nodders, or Bobblehead dolls as they are commonly known, I saw half a dozen listings for Santa Nodders from different countries. They were all listed by the same seller at the same time, each with a starting price of $9.99. None of them had sold. Because the Christmas holidays had just passed, it was obvious to me why there were no takers. This seller might have had better luck if he'd held onto his inventory until the fall when people are thinking about the Christmas holidays again.

The Sellers Say . . .

Beth says, "I've looked and have decided there's no correlation between listing time and selling price. My advice: list when it is convenient for you and research items before listing. Don't put something on when ten items exactly like it didn't sell."

Kathy says, "I list seven days a week. I start my listings at 9:00 P.M. Central Time so I reach the East Coast at 10:00 P.M and the West Coast at 7:00 P.M."

Scott says, "We list on Thursday and Saturdays starting at 6:00 P.M. Every once in a while we will list on Thursday or Sunday. Never Monday. It has been our experience that those are the best days to sell."

Cindy says, "I used to list only evening auctions and try to have the best items ending on Sunday night. But I have found with the Buy It Now that isn't as important as it used to be."

Jane says, "My listings always end at night when most people are home after supper, but time zone is a consideration, too. Weekends seem to do better, but I list every day except Monday."

SPOTLIGHT ON NODDERS

In 1961, Nodders were produced in the likeness of baseball greats Mickey Mantle, Roger Maris, Willie Mays, and
Roberto Clemente. This is the first time the bobbleheads looked like
a particular person. The idea caught on, and through the 1960s and
1970s, you could find Nodders for not only athletes but also cartoon
characters like Popeye, holiday figures like Santa, and famous people like the Beatles.

In 2006, modern technology makes the production of Nodders an
easy task. With three photos (front, back, and side) of a person, the
computer can generate a mold for a Nodder that truly resembles
that person. An eBay search found 1,117 current listings for Nodders
and 2,459 completed listings. A huge array of figures were available. The ones that were the most marketable, however, were definitely the sport figure Nodders. A papier-mache Kansas City Chiefs
doll from the 1960s sold for $179.50 and a Miami Dolphins figure
went for $94.13.

CHAPTER 7

Customer
Care

*I*F YOU'RE GOING TO SUCCEED SELLING ON EBAY, YOU
need to take care of your buyers. Most of
them know what they're looking for and have a
good sense of its value, and they expect good service as part of the
bargain. Bidders often ask a lot of questions and want fast answers.

An aspect unique to online auctions is the feedback system, where
both buyers and sellers can leave comments about one another
that are visible to all other eBay users. Providing poor customer
service puts you at risk of negative feedback, which could have a
serious impact on your sales.

The Seller Says . . .

Sam says, "I often send gifts to my buyers such as a postcard from the area they live in. I always respond quickly to their e-mails."

Though most eBay users are reasonable and honest with the way they use the feedback system, a few use it more as a weapon by threatening to leave negative feedback if they don't get the goods or services they want, regardless of whether their request is realistic. This attitude is referred to as "feedback extortion" and eBay has a firm policy against it that can result in the user's account being suspended. The eBay system allows you to post responses to negative feedback.

How to Provide Great Customer Service

Whether your business consists exclusively of auctions, or you also sell from a web site or even a bricks-and-mortar store, the basic principles of customer service remain the same:

- *See your business through your customers' eyes.* Is your operation user friendly, efficient, and responsive?
- *Ask what your customers want and need.* Don't assume that you know what your customers want; ask them—and listen to their answers.
- *Meet or exceed expectations.* When you promise to do something—whether it's to provide information, ship a product, or something else—do as you promised.

- *Ask if there's anything else you can do.* When the transaction is complete, find out if you can provide any other product or service. A simple, "Is there anything else I can help you with?" can net you additional sales and invaluable goodwill.
- *Keep in touch.* Let your customers know that they are important to you after the sale is complete and you've gotten their money.
- *Be a copycat.* Pay attention to good customer service everywhere you shop and when you receive it, duplicate those techniques in your eBay operation.

The Seller Says . . .

Jane says, "I try to keep communication on a personal level, and I do not charge packing or handling fees" . . . . when I write an auction I try to look at it from the buyer's standpoint, and the first thing a buyer asks themselves is 'What is this going to cost me to get to my doorstep?' I include all shipping fees up front so they know there are no hidden charges. And when I am paid, I provide the buyer with a delivery confirmation number, so they can track their item, and a lot of people really like this."

Communication Is Key

From the minute you post an auction, be prepared to respond to e-mails promptly. Remember, these are messages coming from potential customers or existing customers who may purchase again. If someone e-mails to ask if the vintage toaster you are selling was manufactured by Landers, Frary & Clark, you need to respond to them, whether you know the correct answer or not. Honesty is the best policy, and will probably get you more bids.

If you see a pattern in the types of questions you get asked, look for ways to answer them in your item description or on your About Me page. You can also develop standard responses that you can easily paste into an e-mail and quickly customize for the particular situation.

As soon as an auction closes, send the winning bidder a notice that outlines exactly how the transaction will proceed. Calculate shipping, acknowledge receipt of payment, shipping schedule, when item is shipped, and a tracking number if applicable. eBay has a free invoice system that will automatically do a lot of this for you. There is also a message block to customize the invoice.

Notify the buyer after you post feedback, and ask them to post feedback for you when they have received the product. Follow up with an e-mail to see if he was satisfied with his purchase. Thank him for positive feedback.

Treat all your communications with other eBay users as business correspondence, and remember your e-mails are a

SPOTLIGHT ON LANDERS, FRARY & CLARK KITCHENWARE

In 1912, the first Universal appliance is introduced by Landers, Frary & Clark of New Britain, Connecticut. It was a "thermo cell" electric iron, and was soon followed by toasters, percolators, and electric ranges. This prominent kitchenware company produced thousands of kitchen items including cutlery, bread makers, food choppers, scales, can openers, and aluminum cookware. It had a policy of making its own parts and in the 1920s employed over 3,000 people.

In 2006, a search on eBay for Landers, Frary & Clark kitchen items turned up 71 current listings and 142 completed listings. Many items went unsold, but there were some highlights worth mentioning. A cast-iron Universal churn went for $195, a Hunter's Pride etched knife sold for $89, and a cast-iron coffee grinder/mill fetched $1,025. All three items had reserve prices on them, and all three reserves were met. Since Landers, Frary & Clark was acquired by General Electric Company's Houseware Division in 1965, its products will likely become more and more collectible as time goes on.

strong reflection of your operation. Check for misspelled words or poor grammar. Try not to write anything that could be considered insulting or inflammatory.

Will You Take Returns?

State your returns policy clearly in all your auctions and post it on your About Me page. Your return policy should include a time limit, a description of the circumstances under which items can be returned, who pays for shipping, whether you charge a restocking fee, and any procedures customers must follow to return an item. Will you refund shipping costs if an item is returned? Most sellers don't. If your return policy promises to make refunds to dissatisfied customers, you are required by federal law to do that.

SquareTrade

SquareTrade is a great eBay tool that reduces the risk of problems with transactions. By displaying the SquareTrade seal on your auctions, you are demonstrating a level of trustworthiness, and buyers will feel confident that they will have a positive experience dealing with you. For a small monthly fee, SquareTrade offers buyer protection services, negative feedback notification, dispute resolution, and more.

SquareTrade also offers a sidebar that interacts as a shopping assistant by providing competitive price comparisons on eBay, as well as other online sites. This tool also includes anti-phishing and fraud detection technology by alerting users if they click a suspicious link. For additional information, check out eBay's SquareTrade section by clicking on the Services link at the top of eBay's home page, and then clicking on Buying & Selling.

Importance of Packing and Shipping

Many collectibles are breakable. Your buyer will be unhappy if the item is broken when it arrives at their door, especially if it is something like a bottle of vintage perfume! The care you take in the packing and shipping your collectibles may be the most important task in each of your collectible sales. The last

---

SPOTLIGHT ON PERFUME BOTTLES

In 1927, Baccarat designed two of its most famous perfume bottles. Silver Butterfly by Delettrez was a pink crystal vertical hexagon with silver ornamentation. Astris by L. T. Piver was a crystal star with silver six-pointed motif. Companies spent a lot of time and effort determining the packaging of their new products. A fabulous visual presentation was essential for a perfume's success.

In 2006, vintage perfume bottles are plentiful on eBay. I found 1,120 current listings and 2,644 completed listings. Many listings in both categories had no bids no matter what the starting price, but Baccarat perfume bottles were doing quite well. Many of them sold for over $100 and one 7-inch pink and white bottle went for $495. My most amazing find, however, was a 2-inch Art Deco perfume bottle that sold for a whopping $887.77.

---

thing the buyer will remember is the condition of the item when they received it.

In most eBay transactions, the buyer pays for shipping, but that doesn't mean you don't have to worry about handling this part of the transaction effectively and efficiently. Be fair with your shipping and handling charges. Cover your costs but resist the urge to make this a profit center. Because shipping can add substantially to the cost of an item, many eBay sellers focus on products that are small, easy to pack, and don't cost a lot to ship.

Many eBay sellers say one of their biggest early mistakes was underestimating shipping charges. If you are setting a fixed shipping price in your auction, be sure you calculate it accurately. This is especially important if sending international mail. A one-pound difference can change the cost by several dollars. A decent postage scale is essential so you can quote accurate shipping charges. But beware: Rates vary according to the package's destination. Also be aware that very large packages may fall into an oversize category, where shipping costs can be higher. Extremely large packages cannot be shipped by conventional carriers.

Follow the adage "underpromise and overdeliver," and give yourself some wiggle room on your delivery commitments in case a situation comes up that is out of your control. For instance, deliveries may be delayed due to inclement weather. During the holidays, lower classes of mail can routinely be delayed by several days. Sometimes packages are sent to the wrong address because the buyer neglected to update their eBay or PayPal account. Be sure to check the e-mail for a PayPal payment to see if the buyer has added a message with an alternate shipping address.

Shipping can also be a marketing tool. Offer choices so your customers can select how fast they want to receive their merchandise and how much they want to pay. Consider offering free shipping on big items, Buy It Now items, or multiple purchases, or combine shipping on several small items. Whenever possible, include the cost of shipping in your auction description so prospective buyers can consider that when placing a bid.

Don't Just Toss It in a Box

Your best line of defense against freight damage is to pack your items to travel safely, for example:

- Use only sturdy cartons that can be completely sealed. Corrugated boxes are usually best.
- Pack firmly, but don't overload the box. Cartons should not rattle or bulge.
- Maintain a padded space between your item and the wall of the box to absorb shocks.
- Each item should be wrapped individually in paper or cloth and separated from other items with sufficient cushioning to prevent damage from shock or vibration.
- Pack items in layers, placing the heaviest items on the bottom and the lightest on top.

- Do not pack hard or heavy items in the same box with fragile items.
- Seal each box completely with appropriate packaging tape. Do not use string or paper overwrap, which can get caught in automated sorting equipment and damage both the equipment and your package.
- Label each carton with the name and address of both the shipper and the recipient. Number the boxes in the case of multicarton shipments (Box 1 of 4, Box 2 of 4, etc.).
- Include an inside label with complete shipper and recipient names and addresses in case something causes the outside label to become unreadable.

If you are buying new merchandise from a manufacturer or wholesaler, consider having them pack your merchandise individually (rather than in bulk) so it's ready for you to ship out. You'll have to pay extra, but you'll save on in-house labor and supplies.

Choosing a Carrier

Become familiar with the various package and freight carriers before making a decision on which to use. Lowest price is not always the best value.

Package carriers (such as UPS, FedEx, DHL, and the USPS) handle smaller shipments with per-package weight limits typically ranging from 70 to 150 pounds. Many offer a choice of ground or air service. Common freight carriers are truck lines that handle large, heavy shipments that are too big for the package carriers. When choosing a carrier, points to consider include:

- What are the size and weight limitations, and how does that compare with what you are shipping?
- What levels of service are available?
- Does the carrier offer online package tracking? How easy or difficult is it to use?
- Will the carrier make multiple delivery attempts without charging an extra fee?
- Does the carrier offer e-mail notification to let your customer know the package is on the way?
- Does the carrier deliver on Saturdays and, if so, is there an extra charge?
- How late will the carrier make pickups at your facility, and how does this blend with your work schedule?
- Does the carrier have a facility where your customers can pick up their package? (This is known as "hold for pickup.")
- Does the carrier offer return services to help you retrieve packages if necessary?
- Will the carrier provide delivery confirmation and, if so, is there an extra charge?
- Is the carrier financially stable?

International Shipping

Many eBay sellers don't like to ship overseas because they don't understand the process or find it to be too much work.

The Sellers Say . . .

Jane says, "I prefer Priority, you can get free shipping boxes off their web site, print prepaid labels online and schedule an online pickup . . . . over four pounds, I also offer UPS. They don't give me boxes, or pick up my packages, but I can print their prepaid labels online, and their rates are less than Priority when you get up to the heavier packages. Tracking numbers are free when you print your labels online at both sites."

Beth says, "I have used them all. I prefer USPS and UPS because labels can be printed from PayPal and packages can just be dropped off. UPS is good for larger, heavier items. FedEx is a little bit cheaper but the hassle of dropping it off, waiting in line . . . doesn't make it worth it."

Larry and Cindy say, "We prefer UPS for the items over four pounds, they are insured for up to $100 automatically, for smaller packages it is generally cheaper to ship mail, we usually ship Priority mail because we can order boxes and supplies without any cost."

Kathy says, "I started using UPS six years ago for the efficiency of picking up my orders from my home. That was before USPS offered pickup and when Federal Express catered primarily to commercial businesses. I will be comparing prices and services this year with several companies in hopes of saving money on my shipping costs."

Scott says, "USPS for pretty much everything. Best prices and shipping supplies are free."

Sam says, "USPS. They do a great job even internationally."

But if you take the time to learn how to do it—and for most countries, it's not complicated—you can increase your profits significantly. Willingness to ship internationally can give you an edge over sellers who won't.

The package and freight companies that deliver overseas (USPS, UPS, FedEx, DHL, etc.) have plenty of information to help you understand the procedures and paperwork necessary to ship to various international destinations. Contact the individual companies or visit their web sites for details.

Shipping Insurance

Shipping insurance protects you and your customers by paying to replace or repair items that are damaged in transit. Emphasize with buyers that if they reject insurance, your responsibility ends when you ship the package. Be sure you can prove that you shipped the merchandise, either by using a carrier (such as UPS or FedEx) that will provide you with a

The Seller Says . . .

Jane says, "I wrap every piece of glass in paper, filling cavities with paper for support, then I wrap them individually in cardboard, then roll that in bubble wrap, and lay this in a box on a bed of wrinkled papers and packing peanuts mixed in. Although I have very few broken items, I still recommend insurance, because you never know what they will come up against or if they will be at the bottom of a heavy pile."

shipper's receipt, or by using the USPS delivery confirmation service. Note, however, this only proves delivery of the package, it does not insure the contents.

Some carriers automatically provide coverage for loss or damage up to $100 per shipment at no extra charge. Don't buy insurance for more than you can prove the item is worth; the carrier will only reimburse you for the actual value, not for the amount of insurance you purchased. Documents that are generally accepted as proof of value include a current bill of sale, an invoice, or a statement from a certified appraiser.

Even when you purchase insurance, it's important that your items be properly packed for transit. If damage occurs and the carrier determines that the shipment was not appropriately packed, your claim (or the buyer's claim, in most cases) will likely be denied.

CHAPTER 8

Getting
Started

ONCE YOU'VE DECIDED THAT YOU'D LIKE TO SELL COL-
lectibles on eBay, you must address the
issues relating to starting up your own small business. Will this be a part-time endeavor or a full-time occupation?
Will you run your business from your home or from a commercial
location? What sort of expenses should you anticipate? Can you
do it all by yourself, or will you need to hire employees? What sort
of legal and tax issues are involved? This chapter will address
these concerns and present the "typical days" of our featured
sellers.

Part Time vs. Full Time

One of the first things you need to determine is how much time you want to spend on your eBay business. Some collectible sellers have day jobs and families. They are just looking for a few extra bucks. Other sellers use their eBay business as their primary source of income. Their goal is to make the most money possible. The wonderful thing about eBay is that you can be successful working both ways.

TIP

Remember that selling on eBay is time consuming. You have to acquire the collectibles, research them, write and post the listings, take photographs, answer e-mails, collect money, and ship the items. Attention to detail is very important. Be sure you are adept at managing your time so you have enough of it to do all aspects of the job well.

Location

You need to choose whether to run your business from your home or from a different location. The success of your eBay business does not depend on where you set up your office, but there are advantages and disadvantages to both scenarios. Mostly, you want the location you choose to make economic sense. The costs of running your office need to fit into your business budget. In the end, only you can make the decision about which location will work the best for you and the eBay collectibles business you want to establish.

Home Office

The advantages of working from home include not having to commute and being able to work whenever it fits into your daily schedule. Many of the overhead costs you would pay at an outside location, such as rent, heat, garbage, and electricity, you are already paying.

Unfortunately, not everyone has the space to set up an office at home. In addition, many people find it is harder to work at home because there can be so many family distractions. Leaving the house and going to an office makes it easier to be organized and get the work done properly.

Before you jump in and create an office in your home, check your local zoning ordinances to see if they prohibit an eBay type business in your neighborhood. These laws vary from state to state and it is important to be sure that your home office is a legal one.

Commercial Space

As odd as this might sound, one advantage of a commercial office is that it is *not* at home and there is a dividing line between your work and your family. Your children will not be playing games on your computer when you need to check on your auctions. Your mother-in-law will not be poking her head in to check about Sunday dinner when you are writing a listing. And your new puppy is not likely to jump into the stack of Royal Doulton decorative plates you just bought at an auction. Work is work, and home is home. For many eBay sellers, this is the way that works best.

SPOTLIGHT ON ROYAL DOULTON COLLECTIBLE PLATES

In 1901, the Gibson Girls series, drawn by Charles Dana Gibson, was introduced by Royal Doulton. Other fine porcelain plate series followed, including Dickensware (1911) and the Robin Hood series (1914). People would collect the whole series to display or just pick up the pieces that they liked the best. Plate collecting dates back to the late 1800s when nobility would give plates of food at Christmastime to their servants.

In 2006, a search on eBay showed 2,369 current listings for Royal Doulton plates, only one of which was from the Gibson Girls series. This was a new listing and had no bids yet; however, when I dug back into the completed listings, I found that 15 of the 17 Gibson Girls plates listed had successfully sold for an average of $90. The track record for the Dickensware and Robin Hood series was not as good. The fact that they were both produced at later dates may be very significant.

Unfortunately, a commercial office is a much more expensive venture than a home office. You will have to pay rent and all the utilities on the space. You will still need office furniture and equipment. There will be automobile expenses, parking, and other commuting costs. Again, before you sign a lease, be sure to check your local zoning laws to be sure you can legally operate from that particular commercial space.

Start-Up Expenses

Starting a collectibles business on eBay need not require a large financial investment, especially if you are working from home. There are, however, some items you may need to purchase before you sell a single collectible.

Office Equipment and Supplies

It is absolutely necessary to have a working computer with internet access to start an eBay business. You will also need a printer and a digital camera. If you don't already have office furnishings like a desk, lamp, and shelves to store your collectibles, these will be additional start-up costs as well.

You will need a variety of stationery supplies like printer paper, envelopes, labels, pens, binders, or other record-keeping files. You might also want business cards.

Packing Materials

Always give your collectibles more protection than they probably need. Be sure to seal items that could be damaged by water in plastic and double box any items that are extremely fragile, like glass and pottery. If you are shipping bendable items like photographs or LP records, make sure you pack them between sturdy cardboard to keep them intact. For all collectibles you will need a variety of packing supplies.

Corrugated boxes are a necessity except if you only sell small flat items. You can purchase boxes in various sizes from wholesalers like U-Line (www.uline.com), office supply stores, moving companies, or even from the post office. You can also try to find free boxes at places like your local supermarket or library.

Padded envelopes work well for collectibles like books and other flat items. It is a good idea, however, to prewrap the item in clean paper or tissue before sliding it into the envelope. This little extra care will show the buyer that you tried to protect their item as much as possible.

Packing peanuts come in either styrofoam or biodegradable varieties. They are lightweight and won't increase the weight of your package too much. If they are kept clean, they can be reused over and over again. Consider storing them in large plastic garbage bags to keep out any moisture. If you use the garbage bags with the built-in handle, you can hang the bags of peanuts up and out of the way.

Shredded paper should be easy to come by, especially if

> **TIP**
>
> Save and reuse packing materials as long as they are clean, dry, and smoke free.

you keep a shredding machine in your office. It is an inexpensive alternative to packing peanuts, but it may not work as well and it will add more weight to your package.

TIP

Check out wholesalers like U-Line for buying shipping materials in bulk.

Bubble wrap should be used to protect all breakable items before they go in a box. Even if you are using packing peanuts, an additional layer of bubble wrap helps protect the item from damage. Use bigger bubbles for more fragile items. Wrap around twice and tape gently.

A heavy-duty packing tape is necessary to secure your packages. Buy your packing tape in bulk as you will need a lot of it. A tape gun is also helpful.

Reference Materials

You may want to invest in a few research books, periodicals, or price guides. A personal library geared toward your favorite collectibles will keep valuable information within reach. When you have a question about a collectible, you can find the answer easily without a trip to the library or a time-consuming search of the internet.

Legal and Taxes

As your business grows, it is important to consult with your attorney and your accountant for advice on setting up your small business. You will need to decide if you will be a sole

TIP

Try to put off any expenses that are not absolutely necessary until after you start making money.

proprietor or a corporation. You will need to discuss state and local licenses, tax permits, and any other subjects particular to your area. State laws vary, but you want to be sure to comply with all that apply to your situation. Your local Small Business Administration office can also be a great resource for information. Refer to Chapter 12 for more on money matters.

Rent and Utilities

If you have decided to have an office outside of your home, your start-up expenses will obviously be greater. You will have to rent a space and pay utilities like heat, water, electricity, garbage, and telephone. You will also need to consider commuting expenses.

Ongoing Expenses

Once you've started listing and selling your collectibles on eBay, you will have ongoing expenses. In addition to the ones listed above, you will have eBay fees, packing and shipping fees, and the cost of buying new inventory. At some point, you may decide that you need help, and will have to hire employees. You may also want to acquire additional insurance to protect your collectible investments.

eBay Fees

As we have discussed, eBay charges fees both when listing a transaction and after each auction is completed. These fees add up quickly and you need to determine which ones are cost effective and will help make you money. Use only the features that tend to sell your items to help keep your costs down.

Packing and Shipping Fees

Packing materials can be expensive if you buy them new. This is one area where you can cut costs, especially when you are first starting your business. Try to find free used materials for packing and shipping. Compare shipping carriers to try and find the most reasonable rates.

New Inventory

Your eBay collectibles business will not last long if you run out of things to sell. Try to get the best deal possible when purchasing your collectibles. For instance, maybe you see an old Singer Featherweight 221 sewing machine at a garage sale with a $75 price tag. It seems to be in good working condition. You are confident that you can sell the machine for a lot more than $75 on eBay, but always ask if that is the seller's lowest price. This simple question could make you even more money if the seller just wants to get the sewing machine out of their garage.

SPOTLIGHT ON SINGER
FEATHERWEIGHT SEWING MACHINES

In 1933, the Singer Featherweight 221 sewing machine was introduced at the Chicago World Fair. It was a small, solidly built machine that weighed about 11 pounds. It didn't sew any fancy stitches, but it sewed really even ones. It was extremely portable and very quiet. All of these qualities made it a very popular sewing machine into the 1960s.

In 2006, today's quilters love this old, classic sewing machine for its even stitching. Although these machines are not in short supply, they are still attracting numerous bidders on eBay. The closed listings showed over 50 Featherweights selling in the last two weeks, with the final cost being between $300 and $400. There were also ample accessories and spare parts available for these collectible sewing machines.

Hiring Help

Working alone at the beginning will certainly be the most cost-effective thing to do. Once you start hiring staff, you have to deal with salaries, health insurance, and other expenses. When it becomes obvious that you can no longer do everything yourself, your business should be at a point where you can afford to hire help.

Insurance

At some point, you will want to consider purchasing property insurance to cover your collectibles inventory in the event of fire, theft, or other disaster. The trick is to get solid coverage without spending an outrageous amount on it. If you rent a commercial space, your lease may require a specific amount of insurance. It may also require liability insurance in addition to property insurance. Check with your insurance agent. She will be able to tell you the best way to cover your collectibles. You might be able to add a rider to an existing homeowner's policy, or your situation may require the purchase of new insurance.

Collectible Business Chores

Because each eBay collectible business is as unique as its owner, there isn't a typical day that everyone shares. Many tasks, however, are common to all. Collectibles need to be priced, photographed, and listed. Auctions need to be monitored and feedback given. E-mails need to be sent and phone calls answered. Collectibles need to be packed and shipped to their destinations. When inventory gets low, more items need to be bought. Transactions need to be recorded, and bills need to be paid. Our profiled sellers were asked to describe their typical days. Their responses are listed in the following sections.

Beth's Typical Day:
Collectibles from the 1960s and 1970s

Since I'm only doing this part time, I usually don't devote any one entire day. Things I might do on an 'eBay day' are . . . check my e-mail for questions, payments . . . get all of the things I'd like to sell upstairs . . . look up items to make sure they are saleable, take photos of the items, Photoshop the photos and upload to my picture hosting site, write and submit the listing. On the selling side, I might have to get a box, pack the item, print the label, take packages to the post office. Some days I do everything, some days nothing.

Jane's Typical Day:
Glass and Fiestaware

Post office picks up packages in the morning, so first order of day is to make sure packages are packed and ready to go. I try very hard to ship within 24 hours of payment. I also babysit for a couple of hours in the morning for my two grandsons . . . . Pictures are next, I take pictures, edit them, then finally start writing auctions.

Kathy's Typical Day:
Madame Alexander Dolls

I begin work at 10:00 A.M. I answer e-mails, I see what has been listed and what auctions are ending in the doll section on eBay for the day . . . . I pull orders for my son to pack. I type the labels for UPS. I take photographs of the dolls to be posted on my online store or for eBay auction. I do the listings and answer questions throughout the day via e-mail and/or phone. I check the market again. I end my day around 11:00 P.M.

Larry and Cindy's Typical Day:
Coca Cola Advertising

Get to the store about one hour before it opens, lay out what needs to be shipped. Separate into postal and UPS. I generally do the postal first to get it mailed before lunch time, then get the heavy stuff boxed and ready to go UPS. On heavy days (usually Mondays) it will take till 3:00 or 4:00 P.M. to get everything done. Light days may be done before noon . . . . computer work is done mostly at home, but there is a second computer at the store to work on when there. We do all our shipping out of our Halltown location.

Sam's Typical Day:
Postcards and Old Photos

I spend about two hours a day on eBay, the rest of the time on real estate.

Scott's Typical Day:
Vintage Memorabilia

We get to the office about 10:00 to 11:00 A.M. and everybody has their own tasks. I have a shipper, copy writer, auction manager, and a person who travels to pick up collections. I *mostly write descriptions, deal with consignors and handle the little things that pop up every day."*

You will discover a rhythm to your own day as you immerse yourself in your collectibles business. Experiment with different work routines and settle on the one that is most efficient and productive for you. Although shipping has to occur during normal business hours, many of the other chores related to a collectible eBay business are flexible in when they get accomplished. Get to work and soon you'll have your own "typical day."

CHAPTER 9

Expanding Through
eBay Tools

*O*NCE YOU'VE GOTTEN YOUR FEET WET AND ARE COMFORT-
able selling collectibles in a regular auction,
it might be time to consider all the other tools that
eBay offers to help your business grow. In this chapter we will
explore the About Me page and the eBay Store. Also introduced will
be Auction Management Services, the PowerSeller program, and
several other eBay tools that can help a collectible seller stay on top
of the marketplace.

About Me Page

An About Me page is ideal for a collectibles seller. This is a free page
that you can create on eBay. On this page, you can tell potential

buyers how you got started collecting, what collectibles most interest you, how you started your business, and perhaps an entertaining anecdote or two. You can add pictures and a link to your commercial web site if you have one. Readers will get a real sense of who you are and what your collectibles business is all about. For example, if you are passionate about mandarin garnets, you might include details and photos of your trips to Africa in search of them. An About Me page can foster trust and increase your credibility. Buyers may then seek out your other listings or your eBay store to see what else you have to offer. A well done About Me page can definitely boost your sales.

You can tell if an eBay member has an About Me page by looking for the Me icon next to their user ID. Before you create your own, however, it is a good idea to search out and read a number of About Me pages of other collectors to see what elements appeal to you, and which ones don't. Once you've decided what information you want to present to the world, it is a simple process to make the About Me page. Keep in mind, that you can edit it at any time.

eBay Store

Along with putting merchandise up for auction on eBay, you may want to consider opening an eBay store, which would allow you to sell your fixed price and auction items from a unique destination on eBay. eBay stores make it easy to cross-sell your inventory and build repeat business.

SPOTLIGHT ON MANDARIN GARNETS

In 1992, the first mandarin orange garnet site is discovered in Namibia. These garnets were of a size and quality never seen before. Garnets, which have been around for centuries, were often worn in amulets by travelers. Supposedly, these gems possessed curative powers and would protect the health and honor of the wearer on their journey.

In 2006, a search of eBay shows 242 current listings and 712 closed listings for mandarin garnets. These gemstones represented a wide range of sizes and quality. Some were faceted, and others were smooth. Some were mounted in pieces of jewelry, and many were being sold loose. Completed listings for a variety of small stones showed they sold within a $50 to $80 range. Four large stones, however, each sold for over $750.

According to eBay, you should open an eBay store if you want all your listings displayed in one customizable place; if you want to be able to easily generate repeat business and encourage multiple purchases from the same buyers; if you want to control what you cross-sell to your customers; and if you want to maintain a larger permanent inventory than you can selling through auctions.

eBay stores offer a convenient selling platform for all your eBay listings—auctions, fixed-price items, and store inventory. eBay promotes stores in several ways. All your auction listings will contain the eBay store icon. When bidders click on that icon, they are taken to your store. That icon is also attached to your eBay user ID for increased visibility. The eBay store directory is designed to promote all stores and will drive buyers to your particular store. You will also receive a personalized eBay store web address that you can distribute and publicize as you wish.

The process of opening an eBay store is almost as simple as setting up your initial user ID. The only requirements are that you be a registered eBay seller and have a minimum feedback rating of 20 or be ID-verified.

Any items that you have in active listings at the time you open your store will not appear in your store. But any auctions or fixed-price listing you post once your store is opened will automatically appear in your eBay store.

The cost of a basic eBay store is a nominal monthly fee (current rates can be found at www.ebay.com) that increases with the level of services you desire, along with additional fees for items listed and sold. Store inventory listings are less expensive than auction listings and appear for a longer time. However, those listings appear only in your store and do not come up in traditional eBay auction searches. In addition to insertion fees, as with auctions, you also pay final-value fees when an item in a store listing sells.

eBay offers three store levels: basic, featured, and anchor. All have their own customizable storefront and the ability to list store inventory, but featured and anchor stores include additional services. Here's how the three levels differ from one another:

1. *Basic.* Your store is automatically listed in the eBay stores directory and will appear in every category directory where you have items listed.

2. *Featured.* Your store rotates through a special featured section on the eBay stores home page; receives priority placement in "related stores" on search and listings pages; and is featured within the category directory pages where you have items listed. In addition, you receive monthly reports on your sales and marketplace performance.

3. *Anchor.* In addition to the services offered to featured stores, your store can be showcased with your logo within the eBay stores directory pages. It will also receive premium placement in "related stores" on search and listings pages, which means your store will be placed higher on the page than the featured stores. Check the eBay web site for current store subscription fees.

Setting Up Your Store

You want to apply the same principles to stocking your eBay store as you would a bricks-and-mortar store. eBay allows

The Seller Says . . .

Larry and Cindy say, "The auctions get them to look at the store. The store items are always there for sale, and you don't have to spend as much time listing."

Jane says, "Auctions are best, but stores work well too . . . . It is less expensive to sell through the stores, but does not get the exposure. I find that people a lot of time will buy something from online auction, then they will go into my store and purchase more items to get a combined ship rate."

Kathy says, "I love the convenience of an eBay store."

Scott says, "We sell 99.9 percent of our material by auction as it is the most efficient. We sell a few pieces a year in our eBay store. These are mainly high priced ($1,000 or more) items that we don't think will do well if we simply go the auction route."

you to create up to 20 custom categories for your products, similar to aisles in a physical store.

You may decide to use product-based categories or you might use a more flexible system, with categories like Sale Items, Bestsellers, and Seasonal. Consider having a category for new items so people who visit your store regularly can quickly see what you've added recently. These custom categories can be changed and updated as often as you wish, which is a significant benefit to a seller whose inventory changes frequently.

Your store site should also clearly explain how you operate. Take advantage of the Store Policies page to provide a complete and professional description of your policies and

TIP

Be sure to use your store to list all the items you have in your inventory that complement your active auctions, and be sure to mention your store in all your eBay listings.

procedures. Use About My Store to establish your credentials and provide some history about you and your company. Make sure that each store listing incorporates the same features as a traditional auction with a good title, clear pictures, and adequate description.

Use Your Store to Cross-Sell and Up-Sell

All eBay store subscriptions have the advantage of strategically placing promotion boxes in storefronts on different pages that can highlight featured items, provide special announcements, or be used in a variety of ways to showcase your store.

You also get cross-promotion tools that help you up-sell by allowing you to control which items your buyers see after they bid on or buy one of your items, or use the checkout function after a transaction has ended. You can choose different items to show on each listing.

The tools work by allowing you to establish "merchandising relationships" for the items you list; this determines which items the buyers will be shown. You determine what goes together by designating relationships for as many or as few items as you'd like. If you don't include cross-merchandise on one of your items, eBay will automatically select related items you are selling to display to your buyers.

Understand the Commitment

Your eBay store is open for business 24/7, whether you're awake or asleep. You need to monitor your store closely, answer questions from shoppers promptly, ship merchandise on schedule and as promised, and deal with any other customer service issues that might arise as soon as possible.

If you go on vacation or are going to be away from your store for any reason, you can either arrange for someone else to monitor the site and take care of your business or you can place your store "on vacation" with eBay for an indefinite period. However, you will continue to be charged the normal store subscription and listing fees.

Trading Assistants

Once you have become comfortable selling on eBay, you might want to start selling items for other people. You can register on eBay in their Trading Assistant Directory. People can hire you on consignment or for a flat fee to sell their collectible items. Perhaps they don't have the time to do it. Maybe they don't have the interest. Whatever the case, you can earn a little more income by providing this service.

To register as a Trading Assistant, you must have feedback of 50 or higher, and 97 percent of it must be positive. You also must be an eBay member in good standing and have sold four items in the last 30 days.

People in your area can find you by searching the Trading Assistant's Directory. They can then contact you directly and make arrangements for you to sell their items. Because this is all part of your own independent business, you set your own policies and fees. eBay is not involved in any way. The sales will be done under your Seller's Account and you will be charged all the fees.

eBay PowerSeller Program

If you do a lot of high-volume selling on eBay, you may receive an e-mail from eBay inviting you to join its PowerSellers Program. To qualify you must be an eBay member in good standing with a 98 percent feedback rating. You must also maintain a minimum of $1,000 in sales per month for three consecutive months.

Membership is free and you can display the Power-Sellers logo by your User ID. This gives potential bidders confidence that they are dealing with an experienced seller. Other benefits include prioritized customer service, networking opportunities, and special offers only available to PowerSellers.

Being a PowerSeller can be helpful for a seller of collectibles. People will get to know and trust you and seek out your listings. You may find that you get a lot of repeat business. Once a buyer knows that you sell quality merchandise and handle your transactions professionally, they will want to do business with you again.

Auction Management Tools

If you don't sell a lot of items on eBay, the sales-tracking features on your My eBay page may be adequate. However, if you list more than ten items a week, you may want to consider using one of the following eBay auction management tools.

- *Turbo Lister.* This is a free tool for eBay sellers who want to get a lot of auctions online quickly. It helps you list and edit in bulk, create professional-looking listings, and schedule multiple auctions to run simultaneously.

- *Seller Manager/Sales Manager Pro.* These subscription-based sales management tools are geared for medium- to high-volume eBay sellers. From your My eBay page you can monitor all your active listings and manage post-sale activities. Designed to work with Turbo Lister.

- *Blackthorne.* This is eBay's newest addition to its auction management tools. It was formerly knows as Seller's Assistant, but has been revamped and renamed. It is another fee-based tool that comes in both a Basic and Pro version.

The Sellers Say . . .

Scott says, "We use the new eBay auction management system Blackthorne."

Jane says, "I do not use any of these. I have made my own auction templates in Microsoft Front Page, and I just fill in the blanks. I also use Photo Bucket for a web host so I can size my pictures myself, as eBay charges a fee for every photo after the first one. By using my own web host, I can create a background and drag as many pictures as I want on it for no photo fees from eBay."

Marketplace Research

For a monthly fee, you can research 90 days of eBay's completed listings. Main features of this product include access to average starting prices, average sold prices, top searches by categories, and graphs of buying and selling trends.

eBay Pulse

This is a quick and interesting place to check daily for current trends and hot topics. Search the Collectibles category and you instantly see what the most popular searches are at the moment and which eBay stores have the most active listings that day. Today's top-ten searches included neon sign, Precious Moments, baseball cards, and Star Wars.

SPOTLIGHT ON STAR WARS MERCHANDISE

In 1977, *Star Wars* hits the big screen and Luke Skywalker, Darth Vader, and the rest of the crew become household names. Their popularity was huge, and the mega-merchandising that kicked in before each successive movie guaranteed that over the next quarter century these characters would be found on everything from clothing to toys, lunchboxes to drinking glasses, ornaments to books.

In 2006, *Revenge of the Sith*, the last of this epic film series, is out on DVD. Fans waited almost 30 years for the series to be completed, and its popularity never waned. When I clicked "Star Wars" on the eBay Pulse page, there were 11,268 current listings and 32,646 completed ones. Just about anything you could think of was up for auction—light sabers, clocks, keychains, comic books, trading cards, and figurines. In fact, the variety reminded me very much of the diversity of the Collectibles category itself. Although there weren't many high-priced items for auction, I was impressed by how much of this merchandise was moving.

What's Hot by Category

This is a monthly sales report that rates specific items as Hot, Very Hot, or Super Hot! When I looked at the current month's report for Collectibles, the Super Hot items ranged from antique alarm clocks to Lenox collector plates to Wolverine comic figurines. This is a useful way to keep tabs on the popularity of all collectibles.

CHAPTER 10

Finding Your
Customer Base

*Y*OU HAVE DECIDED ON WHAT COLLECTIBLES YOU WANT TO
sell. Now you need to take some time to
determine the people who will purchase these
items. If, for example, you are selling Militaria, then most likely the
majority of your customers will be male. Many of them may have
served in one of the armed forces. On the other hand, if you are
specializing in Decorative Kitchenware, the odds are that most of
your customers will be female. These are not meant to be sexist
statements, but rather the way of the collectible world.

In general, most collectors are well educated and affluent. They are
looking for good quality items, and they know them when they find
them.

Many collectors seek items from their childhood, which, at the time of this printing, means collectibles from the 1950s to the 1980s. Your primary task, as the seller, is to find these customers or have them find you on eBay.

Why Will a Customer Buy from You?

As a seller, it is important to make yourself stand out from all the other sellers on eBay. In previous chapters, we have touched on the qualities of a good seller, but it never hurts to reinforce these ideas. To be memorable to a buyer, you need to try to exceed their expectations, carry only quality merchandise, conduct your auctions and eBay store professionally, be honest and reputable, and take wonderful care of your customers. These things will leave a lasting impression on your buyers, and they will want to do business with you again and again.

I asked our profiled sellers what specific attributes they have that makes them a successful eBay seller. Their responses follow.

BETH SAYS,

> *Honesty in describing the item, even if it lowers the selling price, fast shipping, being willing to immediately correct any mistake. Ship items as well packed as you would like to receive them.*

JANE SAYS,

> *I try to keep communication on a personal level, and I do not charge packing or handling fees . . . . When I write an auction*

I try to look at it from the buyer's standpoint . . . . I include all shipping fees up front so they know there are no hidden charges. And when I am paid, I provide the buyer with a delivery confirmation number, so they can track their item.

KATHY SAYS,

My ability to take terrific photos, the consistent quality of my products, quick shipping, and the personal relationships I establish with my customers.

LARRY AND CINDY SAY,

We ship fast, pack well, price fairly. We don't gouge shipping prices. And, when there is a problem, we try to satisfy the customer the best we can.

SCOTT SAYS,

We just always try to have nice material and a variety of it. The attribute that makes us most successful is how we treat our consignors. The material sells itself, getting a hold of the material is the real challenge, and keeping our consignors happy is the key to success.

eBay Promotional Tools

There are ample opportunities within eBay itself to help you market and promote not only your listings, but your entire collectible business as a whole. Features to take advantage of are the gallery option, the About Me page, multiple category listings, longer running listings, and banner ads.

About Me Page

The importance of an About Me page for a collectible seller cannot be underestimated. In addition to being the perfect place to introduce yourself personally, it also provides the

SPOTLIGHT ON PINBALL MACHINES

In 1947, the flipper was added to pinball machines. During the Depression years, pinball had been popular because it was low-cost entertainment. With the invention of the flipper, people's interest in these games was renewed once more. The "Golden Age of Pinball" lasted from 1948 to 1958. The machines at this time had wooden legs and wooden rails on the sides. They also had lighted scoring levels built into the back glass with a separate bulb for each score.

In 2006, Stern Pinball in Melrose Park, Illinois, is the last manufacturer and designer of pinball machines. The older machines are still popular collectibles selling for thousands of dollars on eBay. The Addams Family Pinball Machine seemed to be the most consistently popular when I checked the completed listings. Four of them had sold over a two-week span for between $2,500 and $3,500. The top sale of the day, however, went to William's Medieval Madness, which fetched $5,500.

opportunity to advertise your collectibles business. When I looked for an eBay Seller who specialized solely in pinball machines, I found one very quickly by reading the Me icons in the pinball listings. I'm sure there are plenty of potential buyers out there doing the same thing.

Multiple Category Listings

Consider listing your items in more than one eBay category. The cost is higher, but you may connect with an entirely new group of potential buyers this way. This method works particularly well if you have a crossover type of collectible. For example, maybe your interest is political memorabilia relating to former President Bill Clinton. Currently, you have a 53rd Presidential Inauguration T-shirt to sell. To reach as many buyers as possible, you would probably want to list it under both Political Memorabilia and Clothing, Shoes, and Accessories.

Longer Running Listings

If you have an item that you think will get a lot of attention, consider running your auction for ten days, rather than seven

The Seller Says . . .

Jane says, "If I have several items that are similar, say for example toy cast iron soldiers, I will list all of them . . . at one time, and I will list some under Collectibles, Metalware, Cast Iron, and others under Toys, Vintage Toys, Cast Iron. This gives you the exposure of two areas."

SPOTLIGHT ON POLITICAL MEMORABILIA

In 1960, John F. Kennedy ran for President of the United States. He was the youngest man and the first Catholic ever elected to that office. Although there had always been campaign advertising in the past, Kennedy's good looks and charming personality made him the perfect political poster boy. His picture was plastered on posters and pins and in newspapers across the country.

In 2006, a search on eBay pulled up only 10 current listings and 22 completed ones for Political Memorabilia. Most of them were for campaign pins touting one candidate or another. There didn't seem to be too much interest, but then this is not an election year. Timing could definitely be a factor. In the closed listings, there was a First Ladies cookbook that sold for $5.22, a Bill Clinton watch that sold for $4.95, and a lot of five JFK pins with an election poster that fetched $20.50.

or less. The few extra days will allow more people to view your listing and, hopefully, bid on it. Sometimes an item can benefit from those few extra days.

Gallery Options

For an additional fee, you can add your item's picture to the eBay Gallery. Not only do you have a thumbnail picture of

the item in the Gallery, but it also appears next to your listing. This makes your listing stand out more. Those who do
not pay the additional fee get only a small camera icon next
to their listing. Potential buyers must click on your listing to
see any photos of the item.

Banner Ads

Through the eBay Keywords program, you can place adver-
tisements for your products or your eBay store above the regular eBay listings. As the seller, you pay a fee each time someone
clicks on your advertisement. People who are not interested in
your product won't click on it, so you are only paying for
potential customers.

Create Your Personal Web Site

If you don't already have one, a personal web site is a great
way to advertise your business. You can sell to customers
directly from there, or direct them to your eBay auctions. A
link between the two sites can be established and you can create a button that says "Click Here to See My eBay Auctions."
Computer software like FrontPage is available to help you
design your own web site or, if your budget allows, you can
hire a web page designer to do it for you.

Take Out an Ad

If you've been researching and keeping up with your collectibles, you may be receiving newsletters and magazines

specific to your interests. Consider placing an advertisement in these periodicals. For example, if you collect postage stamps, you might want to investigate advertising in *Stamp Collector* magazine or *Linn's Stamp News*. Be sure to mention

SPOTLIGHT ON POSTAGE STAMPS

In 1930, the United States Postal Service issued a $2.60 stamp with an image of the Graf Zeppelin on it. It was intended as a promotional item for collectors and had a limited availability. During the two months or so it was on sale, 61,296 of these stamps were purchased. It is one of the few American postage stamps that is rare and quite valuable.

In 2006, interest in stamp collecting has grown so much over the years that it is now one of the world's most popular hobbies. In the United States alone, it is estimated that there are up to 20 million people who enjoy this activity. If any of them are looking for postage stamps, they should definitely visit eBay. A search showed 2,211 current listings and 4,974 completed for new and used stamps from around the world. On the one hand, mint Bugs Bunny postage stamp sets (ten 32-cent stamps) were selling for around $5. At the other end of the spectrum, 11 full mint sheets of Nazi era postage stamps had sold for $250.

your eBay user ID and what types of items you offer on eBay. Collectors who are interested in your specialty may visit you online.

Build a Customer Mailing List

The longer you are in business, the more contacts you will have. If you consistently provide quality merchandise and good customer service, then you will probably see repeat customers. Keep their e-mail and mailing addresses so you can send out notifications when you are listing something that they might be interested in viewing. This works particularly well if you have a specialty. Be sure to ask ahead of time if they would like to receive these e-mails or mailings from you. A great time to ask permission is immediately after the feedback process has been completed on a sale.

Never send e-mails to people you have not had a transaction with on eBay. This is considered spamming, and you could be reported for the practice. Do not send marketing e-mails more than once every couple of weeks. You want to attract buyers, not annoy them. Keep your message short and to the point. Enclose the links to your eBay listings. Your tone can be chatty or businesslike, but keep it the same each time you

The Seller Says . . .

Jane says, "I have had so many people express gratitude for finding that special piece of china that they have been searching for."

send a notification. Be sure to send your e-mails in small groups so they are not considered spam, or unsolicited e-mails.

Pay attention to your customers' interests. Know what specific items they are looking for to add to their collections. Keep an eye out for these items when you are at estate sales, flea markets, or auctions. You never know when they might turn up.

Networking with Other Collectors and Sellers

In addition to keeping in contact with your customers, network with other collectible sellers. Visit the eBay Chat Rooms. Join online groups that specialize in your items. Get to know your competition. These people can also be your friends. You might even end up trading links to each other's web sites.

Once a year there is a three-day convention called eBay Live! More than 10,000 people attend this event, which hosts hundreds of exhibits, classes, labs, and discussions. This opportunity may be exactly what you need to get ideas on how to make your business grow. It would also give you a chance to meet and network with other eBay entrepreneurs.

Keeping Track of
Your Collectibles

*F*ROM THE BEGINNING, IT IS IMPERATIVE THAT YOU KEEP organized records of your collectible inventory. You must always know exactly what collectibles you have and at what stage in the selling process each one is at. It is a matter of personal choice whether you decide on a manual system or a computer software system—just be sure you keep records consistently.

Purchasing Collectibles

As you buy each of your collectibles, you will want to mark down important pieces of information for future reference. Record the name of the item, date and place you purchased it, cost of the collectible, and a brief description of the item including any flaws or features that might affect the collectible's value. If you have a very large inventory, you might want to assign each collectible a number. Lastly, consider photographing each collectible as you acquire it.

SPOTLIGHT ON RIIHIMAEN LASI OY GLASS

In 1959, designer Tamara Aladin joined the Finnish company Riihimaen Lasi Oy. This company's style of glass had clean-lined geometric forms with little decoration on the surface. The colors were bright jewel tones and they used molds to ensure consistency of form and color. Aladin, along with other designers of this era, reflected the "Pop" style of the 1960s in their glass designs.

In 2006, although an eBay search only brought up 18 current listings for Riihimaen glass, there were 245 completed listings. There were no Tuulikki vases listed in either place, but I found two similarly shaped glasses from the 1960s in the completed section. Both had sold for just over $43 a piece. As this style of glass fits in well with modern interiors, collectors who are interested in Scandinavian design may be on the lookout for this type of glassware. Riihimaen Lasi Oy pieces combine quality, beauty, and workmanship.

Name of the Item

When tracking the name of the item, use the name given by the manufacturer if possible. If you don't have that information, temporarily name the item yourself by using the most important keywords that describe it. Later, after you've researched the collectible, you may find the accurate name and can then change your own records to reflect this new information.

Perhaps you see an unusual blue glass vase at a flea market. Something tells you that you've seen this type of geometrically shaped glassware in one of your collectibles price guides. Taking a chance, you pick it up for a couple of dollars. When you get home, you log it in naming it "Geometric Blue Glass Vase," and store it safely up on some shelving. Before listing it, you do a little research and find out that it is really a Riihimaen Lasi Oy vase from the 1960s. Now you can change the title in your records to "Riihimaen Lasi Oy Blue Tuulikki Vase" and hope you'll be able to sell it for $40 to $60, as it is listed in your price guide.

Date and Place Purchased

It is impossible to remember where and when you bought every collectible in your inventory. The date is particularly important when you are gathering information for tax purposes. Knowing where you got an item could also be helpful if a potential buyer has a question you can't answer about a piece. You might be able to backtrack and get that information from the person who sold it to you. In addition, you will want to add that seller into your database for possible future networking.

Price Paid

How much you paid for the collectible will influence what starting price you put on your listing for that item. If it was an inexpensive piece, you can start the bidding very low, and let the auction take care of itself. On the other hand, if it was a particularly expensive piece, you should consider adding a reserve price to protect your investment. While recording this information, you might also want to note an estimated sales value. Once your auction of the item is complete, you can see how accurate your estimation was. Hopefully, over time, you will get better and better at determining the probable range of final sale prices.

> **TIP**
>
> Remember to get and keep all your receipts for tax purposes.

Description

In your item description, be as detailed as possible about the collectible. Be sure to include features like size, weight, color, manufacturer, date, and identifying marks. Also include an accurate appraisal of its condition, noting scratches, chips, or other flaws that might affect a selling price. For example, if you collect lead toy soldiers, you will want to determine the

SPOTLIGHT ON LEAD TOY SOLDIERS

In 1924, the company Barclay was founded by two brothers in Hoboken, New Jersey. Eventually, this company became the largest manufacturer of toy soldiers in the United States, specializing in models of the U.S. armed forces, mostly in action. Over the years, many other types of soldiers were developed, including a "podfoot figure" that occurred when the lead bases of the soldiers were removed and the feet widened. Barclay continued production of toy soldiers until 1971.

In 2006, a search on eBay for lead toy soldiers brought up 892 current listings, 153 of which were Barclay products. It was encouraging to see that almost every Barclay soldier had bids on it. The bidding on one mint soldier riding a motorcycle was already over $86 with two days left on the auction. Checking back, this soldier had ended the auction with 25 bids and a final sale price of $212.50. I also found a completed listing for an officer on a horse that sold for $81. A common sale price for the Barclay soldiers was in the $20 to $30 range.

condition of the paint. Collectors will not mind some flaking, as long as it is the original paint.

If your collectible has a feature that might increase its value, you want to be sure you make note of that, too. Do you have a Certificate of Authenticity? Is there an autograph?

Is there any provenance, special background, or historical information that you can include in the eBay listing? Write down as much information as you have about the item. It will make your listing on that collectible much more complete.

Photographs

Pictures are optional for your records, but do consider them for larger or valuable inventories. They can be useful particularly in case of fire or theft when you might be submitting an insurance claim. In fact, the insurance company may insist on it.

Storage for Collectibles

Your collectibles need to be kept in a safe place until you sell them. If breakable, they need to be kept away from high traffic areas where they could be disturbed and broken. Shelving, cabinets, or storage containers are all good options depending on the collectibles that you have. When you are deciding where and how to store them, think about whether you'll need to invest in an air conditioner or dehumidifier. Some collectibles are easily damaged by changes in temperature or humidity. In addition, keep your collectibles storage area free of smoke.

> **TIP**
>
> Keep similar records for your own personal collectibles. You never know when you'll decide to sell some of them.

The Sellers Say . . .

Jane says, "I have totes, each tote is numbered, and I have what is in totes listed on paper."

Beth says, "I don't have that much inventory so I just try to keep similar items together."

Staying Organized

As soon as you start selling your collectibles on eBay, you need to be able to track when each one was sold and to whom. As with purchasing, only you can determine whether a manual system or a computer software system will work best for your particular situation.

Sale Information

As you begin selling, you will want to keep track of the names and addresses of the buyers, the date of each transaction, what items they purchased, and at what price. You'll also need to note the payment method and when the items were shipped by you and received by the buyer.

Buyer Information

At a minimum, you will want to have each buyer's full name, street address, telephone number, and e-mail address. You have to be able to contact them in case of questions or problems. This information can also be useful for future marketing purposes.

Date and Items Purchased

It is important to have the full purchase date, including the year, in your sales records. This is necessary to keep accurate records for tax purposes. Use the same name you listed in your records when you bought it. List the sale price for each item and the shipping costs as well.

Payment Method

Note whether the buyer paid by check, credit card, money order, or through PayPal. Keeping payment method records can help you see which methods are the most popular with your buyers. Make sure to highlight if there were any problems with particular types of payment. You might decide to stop taking checks if you have too many of them that bounce.

If a customer refuses to pay for an item, you can stop this customer from bidding on future auctions with the eBay feature that blocks bidders.

The Seller Says . . .

Scott says, "We had a person design an accounting program for us to help with inventory."

Shipping Method

Note which carrier was used and the total shipping costs. Write the tracking number for each package and whether insurance was taken out on the item. Note the day you shipped the parcel and the day it was received by your buyer. Accurate records will help you resolve any potential disputes. Buyers will not be able to claim that "the package never arrived." If you print your labels from PayPal, delivery confirmation is free for priority mail and only 14 cents for other types of mail.

The Seller Says . . .

Jane says, "Never ship out anything without a tracking number. Items can get lost, and I have ran into unscrupulous buyers who say they did not receive their package when in fact it had been received, and was documented through tracking number."

Feedback

Hopefully, all your buyers will leave positive feedback for you on eBay after the transaction is over. If you are unfortunate enough to get negative or even neutral feedback, consider noting these remarks in your records. It is important that you address any feedback issues promptly. If you were the one at fault in the situation, try to improve your services in the future to avoid any more negative feedback. If the negative feedback was unwarranted, you can try to have the buyer retract it. You can also respond to negative feedback to give your side of the story. Positive feedback is important for both buyers and sellers.

CHAPTER 12

Money
Matters

*T*HIS CHAPTER WILL COVER THE BASIC MONEY MATTERS
you must address when starting your own
eBay business. The topics will include how to choose
a legal form of business, how to keep track of income and expenses,
the different types of record-keeping and financial statements, and
taxes. Other issues addressed will be controlling expenses and forecasting for the future.

Choosing a Legal Form of Business

Your collectibles business will fall into one of the basic legal types
of business structures available. These include sole proprietorship,

partnership, limited liability company, or corporation. The structure you choose to use is best determined by the number of owners and what types of services or products you will provide. Alone or with the help of your accountant or attorney, you need to determine which legal form of business is right for your situation.

Sole Proprietor

A sole proprietorship is the simplest and least expensive form of business to set up. You are the one and only owner of your business. You make all the profits and are completely liable if something goes wrong. You and your business are legally one and the same. For many eBay sellers, particularly at the beginning, this is the best way to go. As your collectibles business grows, you can look into changing your business structure.

Partnership

If your eBay company will have more than one owner, by definition you have a partnership. In a general partnership, all partners share fully in the responsibilities of running the company. They share all of the profits and all of the liability. In a limited partnership, one or more partners takes a passive role. They may contribute financially, but are not involved in the daily running of the business. In this case, the limited partners are not liable for business debt, although they do run the risk of losing whatever they have invested in the company.

Perhaps you would like to open a business that specializes in vintage Seth Thomas clocks. You have space in your home for an office and inventory. You have the time necessary to

---

SPOTLIGHT ON SETH THOMAS CLOCKS

In 1924, Seth Thomas introduced a new line of banjo clocks. As the longest established clockmakers in the United States, their name became a symbol of value and excellence in craft. Over the years, this company mass-produced quality grand-father clocks, mantle clocks, wall clocks, alarm clocks, and many other types of timepieces from their factory in Thomaston, Connecticut.

In 2006, Seth Thomas clocks are still appreciated today. Of the 3,347 vintage clock current listings I found on eBay, 608 of them were this brand. Most listings had several bids on them and many items had offers well over $100. There was a parlor clock in a rosewood veneer case that had 16 bids and was currently at $456. There was also a miniature lyre-shaped banjo clock with 15 bids and a current price of $380. When I checked back, the parlor clock had fetched $565 and the banjo clock $421. The completed listings showed 1,191 Seth Thomas clocks with 19 selling in the $500 to $600 range.

TIP

Hire the legal and tax assistance you need to set your small business up properly.

run the business. Unfortunately, the one thing you do not have is the cash necessary to purchase the clocks for your inventory. Your father offers to give you the cash but, because he is retired and living in Florida, he is not interested in being involved in the business in any other way. In this situation, you could set up a limited partnership.

Limited Liability Company (LLC)

A LLC business structure combines the pass-through taxation of a sole proprietor or partnership with the same kind of protection against personal liability that a corporation offers. A LLC is less expensive to set up and has less government restrictions than a corporation, but it will cost you more than a sole proprietorship or a partnership.

Corporation

This legal form of business separates the company from the people who own and run it. It is the most complicated and expensive of the legal forms to set up. Shareholders in the corporation are protected from personal liability for business debts, but the company, as well as the shareholders, is subject to income tax.

Keeping Track of Income and Expenses

There are two principal methods of keeping track of your business income and expenses. You will need to choose between the cash method and the accrual method. The main difference between them is the timing of when your sales and purchases are credited or debited from your accounts.

Cash Method

The cash method is the simplest way. Income is reported when you actually receive it. If you sell 12 Pez dispensers in December, but do not receive the checks until January, then that income would be counted in the following calendar year.

Business expenses, using the cash method, are reported when you actually pay them. If you order 5,000 padded envelopes in anticipation of selling large quantities of Pez dispensers, you do not claim this expense until you actually pay the bill. It doesn't matter when you receive the envelopes.

Accrual Method

With the accrual method, income is reported when you make a sale, regardless of when the payment is actually received. Expenses are reported when you receive goods or services, not when you actually pay for them. Using the same Pez example from earlier, you sell 12 dispensers in December. Even though you do not receive payment until January, this income is credited in December. And the •

SPOTLIGHT ON PEZ DISPENSERS

In 1952, Pez dispensers arrived in the United States from Austria. Originally produced as a breath freshener for adults, this product became increasingly popular when character heads were added to the dispensers and fruit-flavored sweets were stocked inside. The dispenser's initial characters included Popeye and Santa Claus. Over the years, many other animals, people, film characters, and holidays have been represented.

In 2006, there are thousands and thousands of available Pez dispensers on eBay. The vast array of characters include Bugs Bunny, the Simpsons, Peanuts, Muppets, Ninja Turtles, Spiderman, and designs related to every holiday. A quick search showed 3,768 current listings, with 37 of those items starting at over $500. One was for a Mueslix character from the Asterix series. He had six bids and the price was up to $760 with two days left in the auction. When I checked back, he had sold for $1,400. In the 10,268 completed listings, the highest priced item I found was for a set of the Crazy Fruit collection (including Pineapple!). This three-piece set had sold for $3,800.

padded envelopes you purchased would be credited the day they are delivered rather than the day you decided to pay the bill.

Record-Keeping

There are several different areas that require their own record-keeping. These include income, accounts receivable, assets, and expenses.

Income

Income is the money you actually deposit into your bank account. Keep records of date, type of payment, amount of payment, and name of the person who paid you. Income can be in the form of cash, checks, money orders, credit cards, or PayPal.

Accounts Receivable

Accounts receivable is money you expect to receive. These are the amounts that people owe you. Examples are checks that have been mailed and PayPal that has not been transferred to your bank.

Assets

Assets are the equipment used to produce goods and services. In an eBay collectible business, your computer would be an asset as well as a digital camera, postage machine, or even your car. Keep track of all purchase dates, purchase prices, and the date these items went into business service. You may have to expense these items over a number of years. You may also need to determine the amount of time these items were used for personal versus business tasks.

Expenses

Expenses are items discussed in Chapter 8. They include everything you have to spend money on to conduct business. Some expenses are supplies, internet access, rent, utilities, insurance, car expenses, and advertising. In addition, any fees you paid to a lawyer, an accountant, a computer technician, or a web designer fall into this category. If you have questions about what counts as business expenses, consult the *Tax Guide for Small Businesses* published by the federal government. You can access it at www.irs.gov.

Financial Management

If you want to build a serious and profitable eBay business, a sound financial plan is essential. It begins with knowing what you have, what's coming in, and what's going out. To know that, you need to keep thorough and complete financial records.

Keeping good records helps generate the financial statements that tell you exactly where you stand and what you need to do next. The key financial statements you need to understand and use regularly are:

- *Profit and loss statement (also called the P&L or the income statement).* This statement illustrates how much your company is making or losing over a designated period—monthly, quarterly, or annually—by subtracting expenses from your sales to arrive at a net result, which is either a profit or a loss.

- *Balance sheet.* A balance sheet is a table showing your assets, liabilities, and capital at a specific point. A balance sheet is typically generated monthly, quarterly, or annually when the books are closed.
- *Cash flow statement.* This summarizes the operating, investing, and financing activities of your business as they relate to the inflow and outflow of cash. As with the profit and loss statement, a cash flow statement is prepared to reflect a specific accounting period, such as monthly, quarterly, or annually.

Successful eBay sellers review these reports regularly, at least monthly, so they always know where they stand and can quickly move to correct minor difficulties before they become major financial problems.

Taxing Matters

Businesses are required to pay a wide range of taxes, and there are no exceptions for companies that sell on eBay. Consult a

---

TIP

Find a good accountant to help you with your taxes. Unless you are knowledgeable about all the latest changes to the tax law, it will be worth the money you spend to have an accountant do them for you.

The Sellers Say . . .

Jane says, "I never pay for packing materials. I go to the different stores in town, and most of them are more than happy to give me their old boxes and packing materials."

Kathy says, "I start my auctions at $24 in lieu of $25. By doing so, I save $.60 per listing. I list about 3,000 items per year, thus saving $1,800."

tax advisor before you set up shop. Keep good records so you can offset your local, state, and federal income taxes with your operating expenses. Take the time to review all your tax liabilities with your accountant.

A potentially sticky area for online auction sellers is sales tax. Many large retailers with online operations have begun collecting sales tax on their internet sales, and legislation affecting how internet sales are taxed is pending at state and federal levels. As a business owner, you are responsible for knowing the law and doing the right thing.

To charge and collect sales tax, you'll need a sales tax ID number (sometimes referred to as a reseller's permit), which is usually as simple as filling out a form. Check with your state's department of revenue for information on how to get a tax ID number.

Controlling Expenses

When your eBay business is first starting, it is very important to control your expenses until you start having regular income. The records you keep will show you exactly where your money is going. Put off any big expenses until you are sure you can afford them. Watch the little expenses like listing fees and the cost of packing material. Do whatever you can to spend as little as possible at the beginning.

Forecasting for the Future

It is never too early to think about the future. Where do you want your business to be in one year? Five years? Ten years? What will you need to do to realize those goals? By estimating your future income and expenses, you can try to create a plan that will help you reach your potential. Dream big, but be practical. Watch the financial numbers of your business carefully to see if what you want is economically feasible.

Hiring
Help

*P*LENTY OF EBAY SELLERS MAKE COMFORTABLE INCOMES
as solo operators, handling everything themselves. But if your goal is growth, you will reach a
point at which you must hire people. This chapter will discuss topics related to hiring help including the difference between an
employee and an independent contractor, how to find and evaluate
potential employees, and what your responsibilities are toward your
employees once they are hired.

Employee vs. Independent Contractor

It is important to determine immediately whether the person you
hire is going to be an employee or an independent contractor. State

and federal tax laws differ in regard to them. You must be sure your employees are classified properly.

Employee

An employee is a person who works for you, on your premises, using your tools and equipment. He works the hours you set and according to the rules you impose. He is always reimbursed for expenses incurred on the job. Depending on the number of hours worked, he might receive benefits such as vacation, sick time, paid holidays, or medical insurance.

Say you own a business that sells old Emerson fans. For years, you have traveled great distances to find and purchase them. After you get them home, you have carefully cleaned and restored them before listing them on eBay. All of this has been very time consuming. For you, the satisfaction is in the hunt and getting the fans ready to sell. The photographing, listing, and shipping are not your favorite parts of the job. You decide you will hire someone to come to your house and you will train them to do these things for you. Because they would be coming to your home, using your computer and digital camera, and driving your car to the post office to mail things, this person is an employee.

Independent Contractor

An independent contractor is in business for himself. He works for a number of different clients and sets his own hours. He has his own work space and owns the equipment necessary to get the job done. He is responsible for all of his own expenses, and must arrange for his own benefits.

Using the same example as above, rather than have someone come to your house to photograph, list, and ship your old Emerson fans, you opt to bring your ready-to-sell fans to an eBay Trading Assistant who lives in your town. You pay it a commission on each eBay auction it runs for you. This person has all his own equipment and all you have to do is drop the fans off. This individual is considered an independent contractor.

Job Application

First, decide exactly what you want someone to do and write a job description clearly outlining the person's duties and responsibilities. List any special skills or other required credentials, such as a valid driver's license or computer skills.

Next, you need to establish a pay scale. This will depend on what you are hiring people to do, the skills needed, and the pay ranges in your area. You should plan to use a job application form. You can get a basic form at most office supply stores. You can also create your own but you should have your

The Seller Says . . .

Scott says, "We were a two-person operation until early 2001. Business was growing so fast that by the end of 2001, I had added three more people."

SPOTLIGHT ON EMERSON ELECTRIC FANS

In 1933, Emerson of St. Louis, Missouri, designed the Silver Swan, the first Art Deco fan. Previously, the appearance of the fans was not the important consideration. Most of them were black and plain looking. As long as it kept people cool, it really didn't matter what a fan looked like. Once companies mastered the quiet function of fans, they turned to the aesthetic side of design. Soon fans became decorative accessories for the home. They remained so until the advent of air conditioning in the 1960s.

In 2006, Emerson currently employs 114,000 people around the world and sells billions of dollars in merchandise every year. Over the years, this company diversified and now manufactures hundreds of different components for electronics, heating, ventilation, telecommunications, and air conditioning. A search on eBay showed 49 current Emerson listings and 146 completed listings. When I specifically asked for the Silver Swan model, there was only one current listing, but the bidding was already at $99.99 and the reserve had been met. In the completed auctions, there were four Silver Swans, the highest of which sold for $273.

attorney review the form to be sure it is in compliance with the most current employment laws.

Every prospective employee should fill out an application—even if it's someone you already know, and even if they've submitted a detailed resume. The application form serves as a signed, sworn statement acknowledging that they understand that you can fire them if they have lied; resumes do not cover this key aspect. You can also compare the application against their resume for consistency.

Where Are Your Future Employees?

Network with personal and professional associates to identify prospective employees—you never know who might know the perfect person for your company. Check with nearby colleges and perhaps even high schools for part-time help. Another option is to use a temporary employment agency. Use caution if you decide to hire friends and relatives—many personal relationships have not been strong enough to survive an employee-employer situation.

Evaluating Applicants

The characteristics of a good employee depend on what you

The Seller Says . . .

Cindy says, "We used to only have a part-time person for a couple days a week, but as the internet sales built, we needed more time to work that. The help does a little of the packing, but mostly they do the store sales and taking internet payments on the phone."

want them to do. If you're hiring someone as a driver, that person should have a good driving record and know the city. If you're hiring someone to help with administrative tasks, they need to have computer knowledge and be able to learn your operating system. If you're hiring someone to handle customer service, they need to know your products and policies, care about people, and be able to react quickly and calmly to surprises. Most importantly, hire people who are committed to giving you their best effort during the time they're working so that your customers receive the best service.

The Sellers Say . . .

Scott says, "I always hire by word-of-mouth. I deal with too many valuable things to hire people that I don't know. The only skills that they really need to possess is that they work well without me looking over their shoulder every day. They have to know how to manage their own time so that they get their work done each week. As long as they do that, I am happy."

Cindy says, "We are very picky about who we hire, we never advertise for help. We don't ask anyone to do more than we would expect of ourselves. We are friends with the people that work for us, more like a partnership than an employee/employer relationship."

Prepare open-ended interview questions in advance. Ask each candidate the same set of questions, and make notes as they respond so you can make an accurate assessment and comparison later. After the interview, let the candidate know what to expect. Is it going to take you several weeks to interview other candidates, check references, and make a decision? Will you want the top candidates to return for a second interview? Will you call the candidates or should they call you? This is not only a good business practice, it's also common courtesy.

Always check the former employers and personal references of your candidates. Be sure to document every step of the interview and reference-checking process to defend yourself in the event that you are subject to an employment discrimination suit.

Once They're on Board

Once you have employees, you need to train them. You must take the time to adequately train an employee. Do you really want them interacting with your customers when you haven't told them how you want things done? Be clear and let employees know when they have done something well and, tactfully and constructively, let them know when they are doing less than an adequate job.

> **TIP**
>
> Consider a probationary period after which either party can terminate the relationship if it is not a good fit.

Employee Benefits

The actual wages you pay may be only part of your employees' total compensation. Though many very small companies do not offer a formal benefits program, more and more business owners have recognized that benefits—particularly in the area of medical insurance—can be key to attracting and retaining quality employees in a competitive employment environment.

Typical benefit packages include group insurance (your employees may pay all or a portion of their premiums but the cost is much lower than for a single person) and paid holidays, vacations, and sick time. You can build employee loyalty by seeking additional benefits that may be somewhat unusual—and they don't have to cost much. For example, if you're in a retail location, talk to other storeowners in your shopping center to see if they're interested in providing reciprocal employee discounts. You'll not only provide your own employees with a benefit, but you may get some new customers out of the arrangement.

Short-Term Solutions

If your staffing needs fluctuate, consider using a temporary labor service as a source for workers when your regular full-time staff is not enough. You may also find that certain tasks can be handled by an independent contractor or consultant. Consider outsourcing work in the areas of accounting and record-keeping, and special marketing projects.

Workers' Compensation Insurance

In most states, if you have three or more employees, you are required by law to carry workers' compensation insurance. This coverage pays medical expenses and replaces a portion of the employee's wages if he or she is injured on the job. Even

SPOTLIGHT ON COLLECTIBLE SWORDS

In 1829, Nathan Ames established the Ames Manufacturing Company in Chicoppee, Massachusetts. Originally a cutlery business, it soon began furnishing large numbers of swords to the U.S. government for military purposes. Swords were used in battle until guns became the weapon of choice.

In 2006, a search on eBay showed 20,111 current listings for "swords." Only 23 of them were for swords from the United States, and most of those were for United States Marine Corp dress swords. The thousands of other listings were mostly focused on Japanese and Chinese varieties of swords, but buyers should beware of scams, especially on eBay. When I focused on "collectible swords" in the closed listings, I pulled up an interesting item. It was a 24-inch Indiana Jones sword with a leather sheath that, supposedly, was used in the films. It sold for $79.99.

if you have only one or two employees, you may want to consider obtaining this coverage to protect you and your employee in the event of an accident.

Let's say, for example, that you deal in collectible swords. One of your employees accidently slices her arm and hand and needs surgery to repair the damage. Because the accident occurred at work, this would be a workers' compensation case.

Details and requirements vary by state. Contact your state's insurance office or your insurance agent for information so you can be sure you're in compliance.

Termination

Sometimes it is necessary to fire an employee. It might be for an obvious reason like they are stealing from you or they consistently don't show up. On the other hand, there are reasons for termination that are less grievous. Maybe their skills are not what they appeared to be in the interview. Perhaps they don't follow through with the responsibilities you give them. Both of these possibilities could hurt your business and you need to address them. It is important to give an employee ample opportunity to remedy the situation but, if they don't, you have cause for termination. Just be sure to document the behaviors so you have a written record.

You've Only
Just Begun

*T*HE FIRST-TIME COLLECTIBLE SELLER IS PLACED ON THE same playing field as the experienced PowerSellers by eBay. It offers access to potential customers around the world and the opportunity to create a lucrative business. You can be your own boss and steer your eBay collectible business in whatever direction you'd like it to go. You can choose to have a low-key venture from your home, or you can expand it into a full-time business with several employees in a commercial space. You can make a little extra cash every month, or you can try to tap the limitless earning potential that eBay offers. The choice is yours.

Collectibles and eBay

Collectibles are the perfect product to sell on eBay. Most are relatively small and can be easily described and photographed. The packing and shipping of collectibles is generally manageable due to their limited size and weight. Many collectibles are affordable even after you add the shipping costs incurred from purchasing them on eBay. Perhaps that is why millions of them sell there every day. eBay is the perfect marketplace for collectibles.

A Worldwide Experience

How many jobs let you meet people from all over the world from the comfort of your own home? We live in an age when collectors can connect and share their passion through a few clicks of a mouse and a few strokes of the keyboard. Over time, friendships can develop from the relationships started on eBay. How exciting is that? Sam Buchanan, one of our profiled sellers says, "I love that I receive Christmas and New Year's greetings from around the world!"

Still trying to decide which collectibles to sell? Keep your eyes and ears open. You just might be the first to discover the next best collectible item. Read the newspaper and popular magazines. Watch television and talk to people when you are going about your daily life. Even when you're grabbing a hamburger at McDonald's for lunch, be observant. A hot collectible item could be right in front of you.

It's Not as Overwhelming as It Seems

Any new experience has a learning curve and eBay is no exception. Expect to be a little intimidated at first. Proceed slowly. Take the time to learn about eBay and to get to know your collectible niche. Don't expect to learn everything overnight. Each auction you list will make you more and more confident in your abilities as an eBay seller.

Beth Titus has this to say about learning the eBay selling process:

> *The whole process of eBaying can seem intimidating at first. You have a low feedback score. Your listings don't seem as good as others. Your items don't sell. It can be very discouraging. But, as you gain experience, your feedback score will go up and you'll get your yellow star, then blue, turquoise, and on up. Then you'll have a really big score—a $1 item you picked up at a yard sale will sell for $50 or more. You'll gain confidence and before you know it you've earned your Power Seller designation!*

> *When you first start out you think 'how can I possibly find things to sell?' Be persistent. Go to as many yard sales, flea markets, and estate sales as you can. Keep an open mind. Train yourself to look for the unusual. Even if you decide to not buy something, look it up in the eBay completed listings. You might see the item you had found, or a similar item. Research, research, research. It's the name of the game on eBay. When you do look something up, always list from highest to lowest, so you'll know what the 'it' item is. With*

SPOTLIGHT ON MCDONALD'S HAPPY MEAL TOYS

In 2003, McDonald's released a "Summer of Fun" Happy Meal lineup. From May to September, it tapped the hottest toy trends and upcoming entertainment properties to try to encourage families to visit its restaurants. The Happy Meal toys included squirting Finding Nemo characters, Barbie light-up necklaces, Hot Wheels cars, 3-D comic books from Spy Kids 3-D: Game Over, and a handheld electronic game from SEGA .

In 2006, an eBay search for these specific 2003 Happy Meals toys produced dismal results. Although there were a few current listings for most of the items, none of them had any bids. When I check the closed listings, the results were no better. Obviously, collectors are not interested in these toys, at least not yet. I also searched all Happy Meals completed listings to see which, if any, of them were currently marketable. The ones that were selling were the brand new 2006 *Narnia* collections in a $7 to $10 range and the 1969 *101 Dalmations* collections, with one fetching $36.50.

I also wandered into the regular Hot Wheels (not Happy Meals) listings and was pleasantly surprised to see that these small diecast cars are, indeed, quite hot on eBay. There were 22,583 current list-

> ings and 53,842 completed listings, with many of them going for hundreds of dollars a piece. It just goes to show you, that small toys can, indeed, be popular collectibles. You just have to have the right ones!

this knowledge, you're almost assured to find high selling items.

The way to succeed on eBay is to know what sells on eBay. I am constantly looking in the completed items. Don't just look for what you have, look at the highest priced item in a particular category. It's impossible to know the price of everything, but you can get a general idea of the type of item that sells. The phrase 'knowledge is power' is so appropriate in the world of eBay.

If Beth didn't convince you, one of our other sellers, Jane Moen, has this to offer:

I have talked to buyers through e-mail that have told me that they would like to start selling on eBay but, for some reason or other, are apprehensive about it. I guess my advice would be to make a couple of purchases on eBay. This will give you a couple of feedbacks to start out, and these are very important, especially when starting out, because buyers are always looking for some form of security. That is what feedback gives them. Then just dive in and do it. Good pictures sell, and long descriptions bore. Let them know up front all of your policies. I would also advise looking at other auctions, and get familiar with some of the policies of other buyers, like shipping methods, return methods, payment requirements, and choices. Selling on eBay is pretty easy, it is like filling in the blanks on a form.

Lastly, Kathy Shaughnessy shares her opinion on the matter in a very short and sweet manner. She says, "I have never found it hard to sell on eBay . . . we were a natural fit from the start."

WOW! Sales

Every seller has those moments when you have a really terrific sale. Something you bought for a very low price completely exceeds your expectations. Our sellers were asked to report on a particularly satisfying eBay transaction. Perhaps one of their comments will inspire you to sell collectibles yourself. As you'll see, each of these sellers finds selling collectibles on eBay to be a rewarding experience.

Kathy Shaughnessy says, "I love my 'WOW' sales! I have paid $15 for some dolls that have sold from $100 all the way up to $2,200."

Sam Buchanan says, "I recently sold a postcard to the Smithsonian in Washington, DC. It was a real photo postcard of Alaskan children . . . . now I can say I have a postcard there."

Beth Titus says, "The best stories are those where someone had a particular item as a child and is excited about finding a replacement. At Christmas you get the stories of children trying to find items their parents talked about. This year it was a Star Trek telephone, shaped like the spaceship. I rushed to get it shipped immediately and it made it there by Christmas."

Is the Collectible Market Strong?

People have been collecting things forever, but since the dawn of the internet, collectors have discovered a new way to locate their elusive items. The hot collectibles may change from year to year, but any items of good quality and fine workmanship will always be in demand and fetch good selling prices. But don't take my word for it. Here is what the profiled sellers think about the collectible market on eBay:

Cindy Brown says, "I think collectibles will always be a strong seller. If not, we wouldn't have two stores full of them as well as eBay and a web site."

Scott Gaynor says, "It is up and down. Many times a collectible area is driven by just a few collectors. If one or two people stops buying a particular collectible, often prices will go down. If you see that prices are strong, it is a good time to sell. Don't hold out, strike while the iron is hot!"

Jane Moen says, "If you talk to antique dealers, they will complain to you that eBay has driven the price of antiques and collectibles down. This could be a bad sign. If they keep going down, no one will be able to make any money off of it. And the competition is fierce."

Beth Titus says, "I think the collectibles market is strong, but it is always changing. You have to be aware of what's hot and hopefully be able to have it in your inventory to sell."

Kathy Shaughnessy says, "Yes, it is strong and, in my opinion, it will stay strong as families, not just individuals, are collecting in masses. eBay was first in establishing a network for collectors and there they have no competition."

■　■　■

So what are you waiting for? The collectible field is so expansive that the probability of reaching a solid customer base is practically guaranteed. Follow your interests, research the collectibles, find your inventory, and then hook up your computer and become an eBay seller. There are collectors all over the world just waiting for what you might have to offer them!

Resource
Guide

Online Price Guides

Use the following online price guides to help determine prices for your own collectibles.

About.com's Collectibles Price Guides

http://collectibles.about.com/library/articles/blpriceguide index.htm

An index with links to online price guides for everything from action figures to toys. Also has link to articles and other online resources for collectors.

Collect.com

www.collect.com

The web site for Krause Publications, the world's largest hobby and collectible publisher. In addition to price guide information, there is access to news, advertising, chat rooms, e-mail newsletters, and dealer and manufacturer directories.

Kovels' Online Antiques and Collectibles Price Guides
www.tias.com/stores/kovels

The web site of Ralph and Terry Kovel, America's foremost authorities on antiques and collectibles. More than 12 of their books are online in a searchable database of over 450,000 items. An online yellow pages is provided where you can find appraisal services, auctions, clubs, matching services, repair services, conservators, supplies, and parts sellers. In addition, you can subscribe to the Kovel's newsletter or purchase one of their books.

Online Auction Management Services

There are a variety of companies that offer listing-management tools. Each seller should investigate these companies to see which products suit their business best. For a comparison of many of these companies, visit AuctionBytes at www.auctionbytes.com, and click on Auction Management.

Andale
www.andale.com

HammerTap
www.hammertap.com

Marketworks

www.marketworks.com

SpareDollar

www.sparedollar.com

Vendio

www.vendio.com

Online Appraisals

Use these online appraisers to get an idea of what your collectibles are worth.

Ask the Appraiser

www.collectingchannel.com/ata

For $19.95, you can receive an online appraisal based on digital photos and a description of the collectible submitted by you. Ask the Appraiser is a member of the Association of Online Appraisers.

WhatsItWorthToYou.com

www.wiw2u.com

Choose from a Classic, Deluxe, or whole Collection Appraisal. Prices start from $9.95. Site also includes some free research services.

Collecting Publications

In addition to the many collectible e-mail newsletters you may find for your specific interest, there are general collecting magazines that you might find helpful. Check their web sites for current subscription information.

Antique Trader
www.antiquetrader.com
A national, weekly magazine established in 1957. Includes articles, industry news, classified ads, Q & A, book reviews, shopping directories, and auction calendars.

Collector Magazine & Price Guide
www.collect.com
A monthly magazine published since 1970. Includes news, in-depth articles, auction reports, and pricing information.

Kovels on Antiques and Collectibles
www.kovels.com
This is a monthly newsletter by Ralph and Terry Kovel. The 12-page format includes sales reports, current prices, and news about what items are gaining in popularity and value.

Wholesale Equipment and Supplies

There are many wholesalers who carry specific collectible equipment and supplies. Here are two general web sites you might want to consult for shipping and packing materials.

Uline
www.uline.com
A leading distributor of shipping and packing material throughout the United States. Carries over 10,000 products

and tries to combine the best quality with the best value. Satisfaction guaranteed—30-day, no-hassle return policy.

PackagingSupplies
www.packagingsupplies.com
Over 5,000 packing and shipping products for businesses large and small at wholesale prices. Will match or beat best possible price.

Online Book Stores

If your local book store or library cannot provide you with the materials you need, search these online stores. They are divided into general book stores and collector-specific stores.

General Book Stores
    Amazon.com
    BarnesandNoble.com

Collector-Specific Book Stores
    Lwbooks.com
    Collectorbooks.com
    Schifferbooks.com
    Krause.com

Book Price Guides

The following are great portable tools to keep in your home library or in your car.

Husfloen, Kyle. *Antique Trader Antiques & Collectibles Price Guide 2006*. Iola, WI: Krause Publications, 2005.

Kovels, Terry and Ralph. *Kovels' Antiques & Collectibles Price Guide 2006.* New York: Random House, 2005.

Marsh, Madeleine. *Miller's: Collectibles—Price Guide 2006.* London: Mitchell Beazley, 2005.

Miller, Judith, and Mark Hill. *Collectibles Price Guide 2006.* New York: DK Publishing, 2005.

Additional Titles

If you want more information on selling your collectibles on eBay, here are three recent competitive titles.

Holden, Greg. *The Collector's Guide to eBay.* Emerysville, CA: McGraw-Hill/Osborne, 2005.

Prince, Dennis L., and Lynn Dralle. *How to Sell Antiques and Collectibles on eBay . . . and Make a Fortune!* New York: McGraw-Hill, 2005.

Wiggins, Pamela Y. *Buying & Selling Antiques and Collectibles on eBay.* Boston: Thomson, 2004.

Collecting Clubs and Associations

Visit www.collectors.org, the official web site for the Association of Collecting Clubs and the National Association of Collectors. You may find it helpful in locating a club that is specific to your own interests.

The following list is a sample of clubs and associations that deal with specific collectibles. It is not meant to be all-inclusive.

American Carnival Glass Association
9621 Springwater Lane
Miamisburg, OH 45342

American Cookie Jar Association
1600 Navajo Road
Norman, OK 73026

American Fan Collectors' Association
P.O. Box 5473
Sarasota, FL 34277

Civil War Collectors & The American Militaria Exchange
5970 Taylor Ridge Drive
West Chester, OH 45069

Coca Cola Collector's Club International
P.O. Box 49166
Atlanta, GA 30359

Folk Art Society of America
P.O. Box 17041
Richmond, VA 23226

Golf Collector's Society
P.O. Box 24102
Cleveland, OH 44124

Hummel Collectors Club
1261 University Drive
Yardley, PA 19067

International Perfume Bottle Association
396 Croton Road
Wayne, PA 19087

Kitchen Antiques & Collectibles News
4645 Laurel Ridge Drive
Harrisburg, PA 17119

Marble Collectors Unlimited
P.O. Box 206
Northborough, MA 01532

National Association of Watch & Clock Collectors
514 Poplar Street
Columbia, PA 17512

National Fantasy Club for Disneyana Collectors & Enthusiasts
P.O. Box 106
Irvine, CA 92713

National Fishing Lure Collector's Club
H.C. 33, Box 4012
Reeds Spring, MO 65737

Pen Collectors of America
P.O. Box 80
Redding Ridge, CT 06876

Pez Collectors News
P.O. Box 14956
Surfside Beach, SC 29587

Royal Doulton International Collectors' Club
700 Cottontail Lane
Somerset, NH 08873

Snowdome Collector's Club
P.O. Box 53262
Washington, DC 20009

Toy Soldier Collectors of America
5340 40th Ave North
St. Petersburg, FL 33709

United Federation of Doll Clubs
10920 North Ambassador Drive
Kansas City, MO 64153

Universal Autograph Collectors' Club
P.O. Box 6181
Washington, DC 20044

Glossary

About Me: an eBay page that informs other members about you.

Active Listing: a sale that is currently happening.

Antique: an item that has artistic and historical value and is more than 100 years old.

As Is: in its present condition.

Authentication: the process of determining that it is original and not a fake.

BIN: buy it now.

COA: certificate of authenticity.

Collectible: an item that someone collects.

Consignment: the process of selling something for someone else.

FB: feedback.

FE: first edition—first in that series.

GC: good condition.

Grading: a system for describing the condition of an item.

HTF: hard to find.

Limited Edition: only a certain number were made and no more will be made.

Mark: a trademark or identifying stamp of the manufacturer.

Market Value: price determined by a willing buyer and a willing seller.

Mint: term used to describe an object in unused condition.

MIB: mint in box

NR: no reserve

PowerSeller: a consistent, high-volume seller.

Provenance: the history of a particular item.

Relist: to put an item up for sale again.

Reserve Price: a hidden price that protects the seller if the bids do not go high enough.

TM: trademark.

TOS: terms of service, including acceptable payment options, shipping fees, and so on.

UPS: United Parcel Service.

USPS: U.S. Postal Service.

VHTF: very hard to find.

Vintage: of old and enduring quality, generally more than 25 years old but less than 100.

XC: excellent condition.

Index

A

About Me page, 13–14,
    99–100, 116–119
Accounting program, 130
Advertising, collectibles fea-
    turing vintage, 21
Age categories of col-
    lectibles, 4–6
    antique, 6–7
    modern, 4–5
    vintage, 5
Antique shows, 33
Appraisals, online, 165
Art Deco posters, 62

Associations
    collecting, 168–171
    membership in, 30
Auction management
    services, online, 164–165
    tools, 108–109
Auctions
    Best offer, 46–48
    Buy It Now (BIN) feature
        as add-on to tradi-
        tional format, 40–42
    Dutch (or multiple item),
        43–44
    fixed-price listings, 42

live, 44
private, 42–43
reserve price, 40
restricted-access, 44–45
traditional, 39–40
types of, 39–48
Autographs, collectible, 24
Availability as factor in evaluating collectible's value, 7

B
Banner Ads, 119
Baseballs, signed, 36
Beanie Babies, 5
Becoming an expert, 29
Best offer, 46–48
Blackthorne, 108–109
Books
    information on selling your
        collectibles on eBay,
        other titles, 168
    online stores, 167
    periodicals, and price guides,
        29, 50–51
    price guides, 167–168
Brown, Larry and Cindy, 20–23
Buchanan, Sam, 23, 27
Business chores, 95
Buy It Now (BIN) feature,
    56–57
    as add-on to traditional auc-
        tion format, 40–42

Buyer information, keeping
    track of transactions, 129–130
Buyer, before becoming a seller,
    experimenting first as a
    eBay, 14

C
Carnival glass, 27, 28
Casual collectors, 2–4
Categories, list of main col-
    lectible eBay, 37–38
Category
    choosing the right, 65
    what's "Hot" by, 111
Celebrity value, 8
Chat rooms, eBay, 122
Classified ads, 119–121
Clubs
    collecting, 168–171
    membership in, 30
Coca Cola collectibles, 21–23,
    97
Collectibles
    as perfect product to sell on
        eBay, 156
    from 1960s and 1970s, 18,
        27
    market, health of, 161–162
Collectors, who are they?, 2
Commercial space, 87–89
Communication with buyer,
    73–75

Completed listings search, 52–54
Convention, eBay Live!, 122
Corporation, 136
Customer
    base, finding your, 113–122
    care, 71–84
    eBay sellers advise on why
        they will buy from you,
        114–115
    international, 156
    mailing list, 121–122
    service, how to provide
        "great," 72–73

D

Damage, common collectible
    condition problems, 64
Date and items purchased,
    recording, 130
Date and place item purchased,
    125–126
DC Comics, 45
Definition of collectible, 1
Demand, 28–29
Description
    detailed, 126–128
    writing your, 61–65
Disneyana, 31
Dr. Seuss book, evaluating
    worth of, 9
Dutch (or multiple item) auc-
    tions, 43–44

E

eBay
    and collectibles, 10
    Express, 48
    Live! convention, 122
    stores, 48
    tools, expanding through,
        99–111
Emerson electric fans, 148
Employees, 94, 145–154
Equipment and supply, whole-
    sale, 166–167
Estate sales, 33
Expenses
    and future forecasting, 143
    controlling, 143
    ongoing, 92–95
Expertise, 29
Express, eBay, 48

F

Feedback, 16–17, 31
Fees
    eBay, 49–50
    insertion, 50
    listing, 55
Fenton glass, 27, 28
Fiestaware, 18–19, 96
Financial management,
    140–143
Finding inventory, 31–34
Fixed-price listing, 42, 57

Flaws
   common condition problems,
      64
   photographs of, 63
Flea markets, 32
Forecasting for the future, 143
Freight damage, avoiding,
   79–80, 84

G

Gallery options, 118–119
Garage sales, 32
Gaynor, Scott, 24
Getting started, 85–98
Gift stores, 33
Glossary, 173–175
Google.com, 29–30, 34

H

Happy Meal toys, McDonalds,
   158
Hiring help, 94, 145–154
Historical
   documents, 24
   value, 7–8
Hollywood memorabilia, 24
Home office, 87
Hot, Very Hot, Super Hot!, 111
Hummel/Goebel, 41

I

Income and expenses, keeping
   track of, 137–141

Incorporating, 136
Independent contractor,
   145–147
Informational web sites, 29–30
Insertion fees, example of, table
   5.1, 50
Insurance, 95
International clientele, 156
Internet information, 30
Intrinsic value, 8
Inventory
   acquiring new, 93
   finding, 31–34

J

Job application, 147–149
John Deere, 21

K

Keeping track of your collectibles, 123–131
Keywords program, 119

L

Landers, Frary & Clark kitchen-
   ware, 75
Lasi Oy glass, 124
Lead toy soldiers, 127
Learning curve, 157–160
Legal and tax advice, small
   business, 91–92, 136
Legal form of business, choos-
   ing a, 133–136

Licensing, state and local, 92

Limited liability company (LLC), 136

Listing
a winning, 59–69
fees, 55
longer running, 117–118
multiple categories, 117
photographs and eBay Gallery, 118–119
strategies, 66–69
time and selling price, correlation between, 68

Live auctions, 33–34, 44

Lladro ceramics, 58

Location, 86–89

Longaberger Basket replacement parts, 46

M

Madame Alexander Dolls, 20, 21, 96

Mailing list, building a customer, 121–122

Mandarin garnets, 101

Manufacturers of collectibles, 10

Market, health of collectibles, 161–162

Marketplace research, 109

McDonalds, Happy Meal toys, 158

Modern collectibles, 4–5, 17–18

Moen, Jane, 18–19

Monetary value, 8–9

Money matters, 133–143

Multiple category listings, 117

My eBay page, 13

N

Name of the item, tracking the, 125

Networking with other collectors and sellers, 30, 122

Nodders, 69

O

Online
auctions, buying and reselling through, 34
interest groups, 122

Organizing, 129–130

P

Packing
and shipping, 77–85
fees, 93
materials, 89–91, 142

Part time vs. full time, 86

Partnership, 134–136

Payment methods, 130

Perfume bottles, 77

Periodicals, placing classified ads in, 119–121

Pez dispensers, 138

Photographs, 65–66
  for record keeping, 128
  old, 23, 97
Pinball machines, 116
Political memorabilia, 118
Postage stamps, 120
Postcards, antique, 23, 27, 97
PowerSeller Program, eBay,
  107–108
Price guides, 29, 52
  online, 163–164
Price paid for item, 126
Pricing, 49–58
  an auction, 54–57
Private auctions, 42–43
Promotional tools, eBay,
  115–116
Publications, collecting,
  165–166
Pulse, eBay, 109
Purchasing collectibles,
  123–124
Purpose of collectibles, 10

R
Receipts, 126
Record-keeping, 123–131,
  139–141
Reference materials, 91
Rent and utilities, 92
Research, 29–30, 50–52, 54
Reserve price auctions, 40,
  55–56
Resource guide, 163–171
Restricted-access auctions,
  44–45
Return policy, 76
Rock n' roll memorabilia, 24
Royal Doulton collectible plates,
  88–89

S
Sale information, keeping track
  of transaction, 129
Sales, Wow, 160–161
Seller Account, setting up your
  eBay, 14–15
Seller manager/sales manager
  pro, 108
Seller profiles, 17–25
Selling 101, 11–25, 15
Sentimental value, 8–9
Serious collectors, 4
Seth Thomas Clocks, 135
Setting up your eBay Seller
  Account, 14–15
Shaughnessy, Kathy, 20
Shipping, 63–65
  and packing, 77–85
  carriers, 80–81
  charges, factoring in, 57
  fees, 93
  insurance, 83–84
  international, 81–83

transactions, keeping
detailed records of,
130–131
Signed baseballs, 36
Singer featherweight sewing
machines, 94
Sole proprietorship, 34
Spending
determining your limit,
34–35
mistakes, 35–37
Sports memorabilia, vintage,
24, 36
SquareTrade, 76
Stamps, 120
Star Wars merchandise, 110
Start-up expenses, 89–92
Starting
bid, 54–55
price, 59–60
Steiff bears, 3
Storage
for collectibles, 128–129
unit buyouts, 34
Store, eBay, 48, 100–106
setting up your, 103–105
understanding the commit-
ment of running your,
106
using yours to cross-sell and
up-sell, 105

what sellers say about opening up an, 104
Swords, collectible, 153

T

Taxes, 92, 141–142
Thrift stores, 32
Title, writing your, 60–61
Titus, Beth, 17–18, 27
Tools, eBay, 99–111
Trading assistants, 106–107
Traditional auctions, 39–40
Turbo Lister, 108
Typical day in the life of eBay
seller, 96–98

U

UPS (United Parcel Service),
82–83
User
identification (ID), choosing
your, 12–13
registration, 12

V

Value
criteria to determine, 7–9
final fees, example of, table
5.2, 51
of items, researching the,
50–52
Vintage
collections, 24, 97–98

perfume bottles, 77

W

Want It Now (WIN) listings, 46

Waterman pens, 53

Web site

creating your own personal,
119

informational, 29–30

What's "Hot" by category, 111

Whiny comments, avoiding, 65

Winning listings, 59–69

Workers' Compensation
Insurance, 153–154

Wow sales, 160–161